AL FRANKEN IS A BUCK-TOOTHED MORON

and Other Observations

AL FRANKEN IS A BUCK-TOOTHED MORON

IS A

BUCK-TOOTHED MORON

and Other Observations

J. P. Mauro

PAYBACK
PUBLISHING

Published by Payback Publishing
45 North Broad Street
Ridgewood, NJ 07450

Publisher's Cataloging-in-Publication Data
Mauro, Joseph, 1965
    Al Franken is a bucktoothed moron and other observations:
    the Right strikes back! / Joseph Mauro and Paul Mauro.
    – Ridgewood, N.J.: Payback Publishing, c1997

    p. : ill. ; cm.
    ISBN: 0-9652966-0-1
    1. United States–Politics and government–1993---Humor. 2. Political satire,
    American. I. Mauro, Paul, 1963 II. Title.

    E885.M36 1996   973.929 dc20
                               96-69350

Printed in the United States of America

Book design supervised by Danny Muro

10 9 8 7 6 5 4 3 2 1

First Edition

to Grandpa

CONTENTS

AL FRANKEN IS A BUCK-TOOTHED MORON

and Other Observations

1

THE MAURO - FRANKEN LETTERS

Johnson, Gladstone, and Miller
ATTORNEYS AT LAW
88 Park Ave
New York, NY 10012

May 31, 1996

Mr. J.P. Mauro
Payback Publishing
45 N. Broad St.
Ridgewood, NJ 07450

Mr. Mauro,

It has come to my attention that you are currently in the process of creating a parody of my client Al Franken's book, *Rush Limbaugh is a Big Fat Idiot.*

It has also come to my attention that you intend to use the cover of my client's book as the basis for your own.

Please be advised that we demand that you immediately cease and desist from any use of my client's copyrighted photograph or any use whatever of Al Franken's image.

Please also be advised that we intend to vigorously pursue any violation of my client's intellectual property rights.

Please confirm in writing your acquiescence to this demand.

Sincerely,

Thomas J. Gladstone, Esq.

Mr. J.P. Mauro

PAYBACK
PUBLISHING
45 N. Broad St.
Ridgewood, NJ 07450

June 10, 1996

Mr. Al Franken
c/o Delacorte Press
1540 Broadway
New York, NY 10036

Mr. Franken,

After receiving a letter from your attorney, Mr. Gladstone, I am writing to you directly to appeal to your commiseration as a fellow satirist.

As you apparently know, I am in the process of completing a book which is essentially an answer to, and parody of, *Rush Limbaugh is a Big Fat Idiot*. As I'm sure you also know, parody works best when one can borrow from the original work. I need to use the cover of your book to portray the idea that my book is a take-off on yours; we intended to alter your cover so as to make our satirical point.

I am hoping that as a person who has been working in parody/satire his whole career, you will not only recognize the importance of borrowing from your cover, but also that you will just be a good sport about it.

I have enclosed some sample chapters of my book to give you an indication of what it's all about. I look forward to hearing from you.

Sincerely,

J.P. Mauro

Al Franken
Delacorte Press
1540 Broadway
New York, NY 10036

June 18, 1996

J.P. Mauro
Payback Publishing
65 N. Broad St.
Ridgewood, NJ 07450

Mr. Mauro:

I received your letter, and I did read your manuscript. Let me first say that satire in the hands of amateurs can be like a gun in the hands of a child. I also want to thank you for your lesson in satire, you really cleared things up for me.

As far as using the cover of my book, I think my attorney has made my position clear. Please direct all future correspondences to his office.

Al Franken

Mr. J.P. Mauro

PAYBACK
PUBLISHING
45 N. Broad St.
Ridgewood, NJ 07450

June 21, 1996

Al Franken
c/o Delacorte Press
1540 Broadway
New York, NY 10036

Mr. Franken,

Apparently, it's all well and good for you to make a career poking fun at people, but I see it doesn't work the other way.

Anyway, I spoke with my own lawyer and he informed me that I really don't need permission to parody your book cover, thanks to something called the First Amendment (perhaps you've heard of it — it's the thing that has kept you out of jail throughout your bewilderingly extended career).

So I should advise you that we *do* plan on using your cover as the basis for ours, and you can direct all *your* future correspondences straight up your ass.

Warmest regards,

J.P. Mauro

Johnson, Gladstone, and Miller
ATTORNEYS AT LAW
88 Park Ave
New York, NY 10012

June 28, 1996

J.P. Mauro
Payback Publishing
65 N. Broad St.
Ridgewood, NJ 07450

Mr. Mauro,

      My client Al Franken has forwarded to me your very interesting letter dated June 21. I want to again emphasize our strong objection to your using the cover of Mr. Franken's book.

      The work is the sole possession of Mr. Franken and he in no way grants you the right to use his intellectual property.

      I want to again warn you that if you choose to violate my client's rights, we will immediately seek a preliminary injunction against publication of your book.

Sincerely,

Thomas J. Gladstone, Esq.

Mr. J.P. Mauro

PAYBACK
PUBLISHING

45 N. Broad St.
Ridgewood, NJ 07450

July 8, 1996

Johnson, Gladstone, and Miller
Attorneys at Law
88 Park Ave.
New York, NY 10012

Mr. Gladstone,
        Injunct this.

Sincerely,

J.P. Mauro

2
FRANKEN FEVER — *CATCH IT!*

When I first heard that someone had written a book titled *Rush Limbaugh Is A Big Fat Idiot*, my first thought was, "well, that was bound to happen eventually." I was actually surprised it had taken so long; let's face it, Rush has tweaked a few noses out there.

But when I saw who had authored the book, it took a few seconds for the name to sink in. *Al Franken?* You mean that old *Saturday Night Live* guy? He's writing *books*? When did this guy come back? I thought Al Franken was dead by now, or still stuck at *Saturday Night Live* (pretty much the same thing these days, I realize). Last I heard of Al Franken, he'd been promoted to doing John Belushi's laundry. Now they're letting him use a word processor? Good God, what's next? J.J. Walker on Bosnia? "Gallagher" on NAFTA? When does Garrett Morris get his book deal?

Imagine, then, my shock at not only seeing the book rise to a spot on the bestseller lists, but at seeing it lodge there, like a chicken bone in a trachea. Suddenly, I was encountering Al Franken all over the place. He was on CNN and in countless ass-kissing news reports. He was lecturing at the White House Correspondents Dinner. He was even made some sort of "political correspondent" at *Newsweek*. The media was parading this guy before me like he was Joe Politics — no wonder the book was selling so well.

I began seeing Al Franken in my sleep, which, I can tell you, is not pleasant. I'd get these hives ... Anyway, it was clear that with this book, there were a lot of media people out there who were going to make sure America knew one thing, and knew it well. And that was — FRANKEN IS BACK, BABY! *And this time, he's got a score to settle!*

THE NOT-READY-FOR-PRIME-TIME PUNDIT

You know how you can be standing at the mirror, torturing yourself over which tie to wear, going back and forth and back and forth? Then it finally hits you — hell, I don't even like these people, and I sure don't want to go to their stuffy dinner party! Screw it, I'll wear the blue one with the kangaroos on it. Who cares anyway?

Reading Franken's book, I had a similar experience. As I was trying to figure out which chapter was the most irritatingly smug, I realized there was a larger, more fundamental question which hadn't occurred to me. And that was: *Is Al Franken really this stupid?*

Now hold on, I don't mean that as just a cheap shot (if I wanted cheap shots, I'd dig up one of Al's old photos). What I mean is, does Al, a guy who wrote for what was about the funniest TV show ever, does he really think this simplistically? Does he really think all these complex issues he raises are so completely one-sided?

You see, all through

CHEAP SHOT: Al Franken, before he became the conscience of a nation.

Rush Limbaugh Is A Big Fat Idiot, Al takes pains to present himself as a political satirist. He *proclaims* himself a satirist like he just descended from some political Mount Olympus. But as a political satirist, Al's supposed to be the guy who holds up the light of truth to all the ridiculous crap that goes on in politics, regardless of who's responsible (and God knows, there's no shortage of ridiculous political crap, on both sides). He's supposed to be out there debunking and exposing, no matter who's gone dirty. Politics *itself* is supposed to be the target. Doesn't Al remember that in its heyday, *Saturday Night Live*'s credo was to play "the loyal opposition"?

But Al's no satirist. He's gone over to the enemy. He's abandoned the objectivity a satirist needs just so he can become another smirking party wonk, desperate as a labrador to please the guy with the leash. And the guy with the leash, in this case, is Bill Clinton.

Of course, after what's become of *Saturday Night Live* recently, I hardly blame Al for deciding to turn himself into the Democratic Party's official court jester. Frankly, after catching a few minutes of his *Stuart Smalley* movie, I wouldn't blame him if he took a job emptying Socks' litter box. But see, I've always viewed conservatism as simple working-people's common sense. And if Al is going to attack that common sense by producing "satire" that reads like one long Democratic Party press release — if he's going to portray every conservative in America as an evil, inbred cretin incapable of grasping his more highly-evolved moral sensibility — and if his buddies in the media are going to keep this noxious junk riding the bestseller lists — well then, don't you think we ought to hear from the other side, too?

And since Gabe Kaplan hasn't gotten around to it, I decided I would give it a shot.

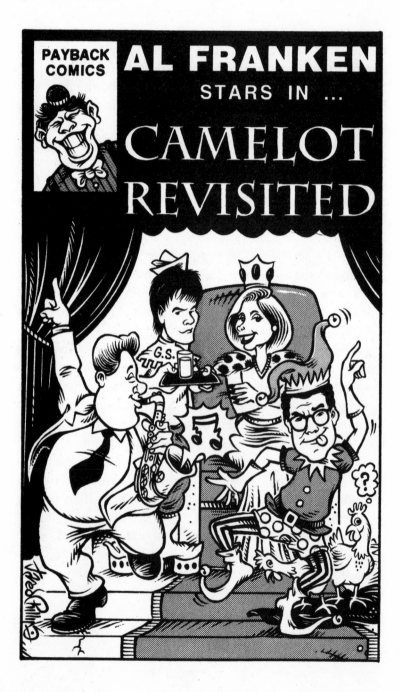

3

THE CANDIDATE CONNECTION

One of the common laments we hear from voters these days is that the choice among the candidates is pretty slim. Voters today often feel that candidates are too much alike, that both parties field moderates who differ on very few things (it's probably this phenomenon we have to thank for the unnerving experience that is Ross Perot).

With Bill Clinton currently co-opting all the best ideas of the G.O.P., many say that it's become so difficult to tell the candidates apart, we're operating with a de facto one-party system. American politics has become like the menu at Taco Bell; sure, the items may *look* different, but try two in a row, and who can tell them apart?

I, however, no longer have this problem. Why? Because I've figured out the one absolute distinction between Democrats and Republicans, the one sure-fire way to tell whether you've got yourself a liberal or a conservative. And it's not their positions on abortion or the cut of their suits. It's simply the nature of their scandals.

Think about it. With the Republicans, it's always skullduggery; back-room-deals-cut-under-the-table, bugging, spy-vs-spy kind of things. Republicans just love to play provocateur. That way they get to be James Bond and Don Corleone wrapped up in one, meeting each other in shadowy rooms in the middle of the night so they can say things like, "Did you meet with our friend?"

"Affirmative."

"Did he make you?"

"I don't think so. I followed protocol."

Watergate, Iran-Contra, the S&L scandal — just a few examples of how much the Republicans like a nice little bit of boys-club espionage.

But if the motivation among Republican males for doing something scandalous is invariably money or power, Democratic males, not to be outdone, have staked out their own scandal turf. I'm talking about sex. It seems that whenever a Democratic scandal manages to reach the ears of the public, it's because some liberal just hadda have it, and he didn't care if he was in a convertible in bumper-to-bumper traffic with the *Geraldo* van sitting behind him. It's a rare conservative that treads these waters (after all, we all know that Republicans don't really have sex anyway, except for Bruce Willis). But what is it with these Democrats? Won't they ever learn?

It's probably JFK's fault. He started all this power-humping. You read any of his bios? No wonder he had a bad back. You would too if you were having your way with the female equivalent of the UN General Assembly. And the Democrats since then seem to have taken their cue from Jack. How about Gary Hart? Remember him? This guy was poised to challenge for the Presidency of the United States, for chrissake. Everybody said he was just like JFK, a fresh face for a new beginning. Too bad he couldn't keep that fresh face out from between Donna Rice's jugs.

Even if they're not married, sex always seems to lead the Dems into trouble. Look at Barney Frank. Here's a guy, one of only three openly homosexual members of Congress. He comes out of the closet, does it publicly, figures he can do some good for the popular image of gays in America. It took guts, it really did. But did his live-in lover have to be operating a call-boy service right from their house? And did Barney really have to ask us to believe that he knew nothing about it?

And I can't get into Ted Kennedy here, as I only have a few hundred pages for this book. But one thing is undeniable: every time headlines loom in the life of Senator Underpants, you can bet there's a heady whiff of whiskey and perfume lingering in the air not far behind.

And so, inevitably, we arrive at Bill Clinton. Now, let's face it. When you first heard in 1992 that there was some gossip attached to the candidate from Arkansas, you just *knew* it had to be a sex thing, right? One look at the guy, and you knew there had to be a Gennifer Flowers in the wings. I mean, what was it gonna be — a bugging thing? Can you picture Bill Clinton trying to jimmy a lock? It'd be like a scene from an Inspector Clouseau movie. And forget Whitewater — that's Hillary's baby. Bill was too busy chasing Paula Jones down the motel hallway with his pants around his ankles to worry about what Hillary was doing with his paychecks.

The way I see it, every time the Democrats want to hold a political primary, they should just dispense with the normal vetting process. Everyone votes for whoever looks best on TV anyway (which, I admit, doesn't explain what Harold Waxman is doing in office). What the Democrats should do instead is just go out and find themselves the liberal-bimbette-most-likely-to-destroy-their-candidate, and let her pick the nominee she'd most like to scandal with. After all, she's going to be the one who will eventually meet the candidate, spend that weekend with him in Aspen, fink on him to *The Enquirer*, then break down on Oprah telling us how "used" she feels while simultaneously plugging her TV movie. If nothing else, this method for choosing candidates would save the Democrats a lot of time and spin-doctoring.

I only wish I'd thought of it sooner.

Our contestant today is the proud recipient of a GED from the State of California, and currently plans on attending Laguna Beach University in the fall, where she'll major in Political Science and nail care. Ladies and gentlemen, please give a big Candidate Connection *welcome to Ms. Tiffany Sweeney!*

(Applause)

Stephanopoulos: Well, Tiffany, nice to have you on the show. Laguna Beach, huh? Very impressive.

Tiffany: Thanks, George. I heard they have nice weather.

Stephanopoulos: I'm sure they do, Tiffany. Well, are you ready to meet our three potential candidates?

Tiffany: Um, yeah. You know, whatever.

Stephanopoulos: Ooookay then. Our three contestants are seated and waiting just around the curtain. You've got the questions — fire away!

Tiffany: Uh, right. Okay. Candidate Number One, describe our first date to me.

Bill Clinton: Well sweet potato, first I'd have you picked up by a couple of my aides, guys who know how to keep their mouths shut, you know what I mean? Then we'd do something cultural, like the stock car races or something. After that, it's over to Wendy's for a nice dinner, and then —

Tiffany: Uh, excuse me Candidate Number One — I don't eat meat.

Bill: Oh. Wow, really? Well. That's too bad. That really is. Well I think they've got, like, this salad bar thing or something. I only use it occasionally myself, 'cause they let you take as much sausage gravy as you want, but —

Tiffany: Thank you Number One, I think I get the picture. Candidate Number Two, let's move over to you. I've become very interested in Women's Studies, and lately I've been exploring my identity as an oppressed woman. If I told you that all sex is rape, what would you say?

Ted Kennedy: Only if it's done right.

Tiffany: Excuse me?

Ted: Er-ah, first of all little lady, my nephew William was cleared on that whole thing. Er-ah, as I've previously stated, we spent a few hours in Au Bar —

Tiffany: Number Two, have you been drinking?

Ted: Why thanks, I'd love to.

Tiffany: Huh?

Bill: 'Course he's been drinking. Does a hound have fleas?

Tiffany: I'm sure I wouldn't know.

Ted: Who asked you, redneck?

Bill: I may be a Southerner, but at least my Daddy wasn't a bootlegger.

Ted: At least I knew my Daddy.

Bill: So did every crook in Boston.

Ted: Er-ah, go get yourself another hillbilly bimbo.

Bill: I'll have you know that I consider nothing in America second in importance to the sanctity and preservation of holy matrimony.

Ted: That's why Gore won't let his daughters anywhere near you.

Bill: That's a lie! I was just asking them how school was going! I oughtta kick 100 - percent of your New England ass —

Tiffany: Boys, boys! Please! Like, e-nough, okay? Candidate Number Three, let's go over to you. If two people are going to begin a mutually-nurturing relationship, what do you think is the most important thing for them to have in common?

Barney Frank: Show tunes.

Tiffany: I'm not sure I follow you, Number Three ...

Barney: Listen, I don't even know what I'm doing here. I think there's been a little mix-up. They said they were gonna be showing C-Span's greatest hits. And where's the buffet that —

Stephanopoulos: Well! I see we're just about out of time, Tiffany! What do you think of our three candidates?

Tiffany: Frankly, George, I think I prefer you to any of them.

Barney: Me too.

Stephanopoulos: Well, I'm afraid I'm not old enough to enter politics just yet! So, Tiffany, who's it going to be, Candidate Number One, Number Two, or Number Three?

Tiffany: Can I see their tax returns first?

All I'm saying is, it might save the Democrats a lot of time to let the bimbo pick the candidate, rather than vice versa. Especially when JFK Jr. inevitably enters politics.

4

A FEW QUICK DISCLAIMERS

May I take a moment? I'd just like to assure you of a few things, and then ask a small favor or two before we get on with the book.

Okay. First off, let me just say that this book was not funded by big-business or the oil companies, and is not part of a right-wing conspiracy with designs on your civil liberties. I am not the point man for some nefarious, phallocentric, Freemason alliance designed to turn the American Constitution into my own personal snotrag. Furthermore, I've never dated a debutante and I've never been a member of the Skull and Bones Society. I was never even a Boy Scout. This book is just a response to Al Franken's book, a book I felt was condescending and not altogether accurate, and a book whose author, in all honesty, looks like one of those Budweiser frogs to me.

There are a few other bases I'd like to cover, while we're on the subject. This book was not funded by the Tobacco Institute or R.J. Reynolds, so please don't send any *60 Minutes* or *Mother Jones* reporters to my house. I don't smoke, never have, and frankly, I think the sight of Mike Wallace might frighten my dog.

I realize this book wasn't printed on recycled paper, but that doesn't mean I am insensitive to the delicacy of our precious environment. So if possible, would you ask Natalie Merchant not to come sing on my front lawn or anything. As I said, I already have a dog.

Let's see, what else: Yes, I do sound decidedly straight, and I will be directing a few jibes at gay Congressman/ truculent jerk Barney Frank. But that doesn't mean I'm not wholly in touch with my feminine side, and I would prefer ACT UP spends its time picketing the White House. After all, *I'm* not the one who told you I'd put gays in the military and is now killing myself laughing that you actually believed me. I would have told you to forget it from the get-go.

I can't afford fur, so tell that Ricki Lake to keep her (still) fat ass away from me.

And even though I work in New York City, and will be pointing out the follies of certain government programs, please don't send Reverend Al Sharpton and his gang to demonstrate or hold a "day of outrage" or anything. I hear the Reverend Al was recently protesting welfare cuts, and said that New York Governor Pataki wouldn't be happy until "we're all in our underwear." If you think I want Al Sharpton on my lawn in his underwear, you're very, very wrong.

Let's see, am I leaving anything out? I want to cover everything. Okay. Let me say that as a white male, I fully recognize my historical complicity in the imposition of a testosterone-fueled domination over the rest of the planet, and I know that if not for me and my kind Earth would be a perfect place and hemp clothing would be available in all major department stores. Furthermore, I am not a CIA operative, and I fully realize that meat is murder.

I think that about covers it. So please ask the following people to remain strangers: Susan Sarandon, Martin Sheen, Mike Farrell, Norman Mailer, Murray Kempton, Marlo and Phil, Mary Tyler Moore, Spike Lee, Catharine MacKinnon, Rob Reiner, Tabitha Soren, Ron Silver, Cornell West, Michael Stipe, Bill Cosby, Ramsey Clark, Don Henley, Daryl Hannah, and the members of Fleetwood Mac. I know they're all very talented people, and I'm sure they can find some other way to fill all that free time they seem to have.

Oh! My publisher asked me to request that they not go to his house either. Thanks.

5

THE LIBERAL MEDIA —
THEY WALK AMONG US

I had an interesting experience recently. I was at a cocktail party dominated by Democrats (don't ask me why — let's just say that my relatives tend towards the bizarre). Anyway, for the first couple of drinks the preferred topics of conversation were the weather, the basketball playoffs, and the weather. It was around drink three, I think, that the place turned into a boozy version of "Crossfire."

Somehow, I was identified as the room's token conservative. From then on, I was the subject of the sort of slow, relentless lobbying one usually associates with an Amway salesman. No matter how forcefully or logically I asserted myself on the issues, I was placidly ignored. Finally, I happened to counter something by saying, "Right — and there's no liberal bias in the national media, huh?"

I waited for the chorus of tolerant dismissals to begin anew, my hosts still endeavoring to humor this unwashed boor. But instead, all the knowing, complacent smiles around me vanished in a blink. Little cups of spring water froze in mid-sip. Suddenly, everyone in the room but me looked like they'd just received a savage, unexpected wedgie.

It was a brief moment, of course, but I'd caught it, and it was delicious (especially since I spent the rest of the evening listening to how the CIA orchestrated the Gulf War for the sake of the Bush family). It was an enlightening moment, too. Because it was then that I realized that, while Democrats will never acknowledge an opposing view on issues like affirmative action or welfare, the existence of a liberal media elite in America is so blatant these days, it's practically undeniable.

Of course they then denied it anyway, and began working on me again with renewed fervor (by this point they were literally backing me into a corner). "Oh, come on now!" and "But you *know* that doesn't prove anything!" were intoned at me from all sides. On and on they came, their serene smiles returned now, frozen in place. *Succumb, succumb*, their glazed eyes bid me. But on a few well-tended upper lips, the slightest bead of flop-sweat.

Why? Because at heart, while they wouldn't admit it, my listeners knew I was onto them. As that sharpest of dead white male writers said, they "doth protest too much." My fellow party-goers knew that I had penetrated to their inner-sanctum, into *the* enduring monolith of liberal power in America.

MANHATTAN'S UPPER LEFT SIDE

Now I know this issue has been covered at length elsewhere, so I don't need to belabor the point. So let's take the nearest example at hand, and have a look at how the liberal media, in just this instance, has influenced what we see and what we hear. And therefore, what we think.

If you remember Chapter Two, I was whining about Franken suddenly seeming to be everywhere in the wake of his book's publication. I encountered that oily smirk of his on CNN and C-Span, in myriad news reports of his hosting the White House Correspondents Dinner, even in his bizarre role as some sort of "political correspondent" for *Newsweek*, a magazine that represents itself as objective press. So let's take a look at Al's media "supporters," shall we?

The first is easy enough. We all know that CNN is owned by Ted Turner, a liberal hustler and the South's least-welcome export since kudzu. Let's face it, anyone who would marry aerobics queen/war criminal Jane Fonda probably thinks Oliver Stone movies are documentaries. I'm only surprised Ted didn't make Franken some sort of "political correspondent" himself — oops, I'm sorry, he did! Turns out CNN hired Al to provide "commentary" on the Democratic National Convention in 1992. Now *that's* objective media. When does Spike Lee get the anchorman gig, Ted?

As for C-Span and the White House Correspondents Dinner, the rather obvious common denominator there is Washington, D.C. In a recent poll conducted by the non-partisan Freedom Forum, the Arlington-based First Amendment group, a full *89%* of Washington D.C. correspondents allowed that they had voted for Bill Clinton (remember, that doesn't even mean the remaining 11% voted conservative; they might have written in Dennis Rodman for all we know). Okay, so they voted for Bill Clinton — but does that affect their coverage?

Well first of all, anyone who thinks otherwise is living in dreamland. But don't take it from me. Here's a quote from a Larry King interview with twitty Canadian and national media figure, Peter Jennings: "I try to caution people that if they're going to look at us for objectivity in capital letters, they're probably going to be disappointed." Peter, you don't know how disappointed.

Oh, and Al's other big promoter? Here's *Newsweek*'s Washington Bureau Chief, Evan Thomas, speaking on the "Inside Washington" TV show:

> There is a liberal bias. It's demonstrable. About 85 percent of the reporters who cover the White House vote Democratic — they have for a long time ... Particularly at the networks, at the lower levels, among the editors and the so-called infrastructure, there is a liberal bias. There is a liberal bias at *Newsweek*, the magazine I work for — most of the people who work at *Newsweek* live on the upper West Side in New York, and they have a liberal bias.

Give Evan credit — he's got balls (I wonder if his pink slip has arrived yet). And by the way, guess who else lives on Manhattan's upper West Side? Yep, you got it — look for the Al Franken statue on Central Park West any day now (let's hope the pigeons take careful aim).

And God forbid a reporter should resist the liberal currents that flow through the national media. Referring to Brit Hume, one of the few Washington correspondents known to lean towards conservatism, Thomas had this to say: "Brit Hume's bosses are liberal, and they're always quietly denouncing him as being a right-wing nut." Well, that's understandable. Brit certainly seems like one of those hair-trigger militia types.

(By the way, in a little tit-for-tat, you should see the review Franken's new employer gave his book. Aside from praising it to the skies, *Newsweek* actually had the brass cojones to call the book "nonidealogical," which represents a break with reality of Margot Kidder magnitude. Not that there's a conflict of interest there or anything ...).

I'm not going to get into all the shrill propagandists who

are still running around loose out there — this book is only so long, and I still have to get in something about Jerry Brown's recent alien abduction. So let's forget Ed Bradley, or that decomposing crackpot Hugh Downs. I think what's more important than fixating on those "journalists" is to ask ourselves this: Just how is this ruling cabal in America's media perpetuated? And can it be stopped before we're all drowning in brie and sundried tomatoes?

THE MARK OF THE LIBERAL

The more I'd like to rouse the villagers, ignite the torches and storm Manhattan's upper West Side, the more I come to the eventual conclusion that it just wouldn't matter. You know why? Because I've discovered something. The liberal cultists are onto us, and they've taken steps to prevent any attempts at reprogramming American journalism.

You see, beneath those serene smiles, they're sneaky. The liberal media has used highly subtle and undetectable means to entrench itself. They're like a small, loosely-knit coven, united by a love of frozen yogurt and loaded dice. And while you and I may not be able to weed them out, believe me, they know how to recognize one another.

How? Think of it as similar to the way dogs ritually-inspect each other. Now, I'm not saying your average left-wing news editor gets down on all fours and sneaks up on his house guests from behind, sniffing at them for their stand on affirmative action (although I understand this does occur around the Sam Donaldson household). With most liberals, these communications are more discreet.

For instance, one day a few weeks back I was in one of America's liberal bastions, Manhattan, and I needed a taxi. I spotted one sitting nearby and headed for it, but just before

I got there some guy beat me to it and climbed in ahead of me. Now, I was pressed for time, so I asked if I could share the cab with him. I'm in midtown Manhattan, and I see that the guy is white, about 40, wearing topsider boat shoes, khaki slacks, a tweed blazer. Typical prep-wear of the well-bred, monied variety. I notice he's holding a *New Yorker*, a bad sign, but not conclusive. I also notice he's munching on something called a "Rainforest Nut-Bar" — it's looking worse.

But you know what the clincher was? You know how they always know each other, in any situation? I'll tell you: it's the knapsack. That's right. You always wondered what the hell was with that little designer knapsack all these characters are walking around with, right? Well, that's why they have it. Not that there's anything in it — it's just a signal. Now, carrying this little turquoise knapsack, this guy knows that should he so desire, he can get hired by *The New York Times* today; he can get appointed by a councilman to a city-wide board studying "environmental racism"; he can walk into a teaching post in the "Holistic Studies" department at Barnard; or he can wander through any of New York's typical demonstrations without getting set upon.

There's more: If he's got a laptop with him, he's a media liberal and multi-cultural revisionist; a valise, an academic liberal or radical lawyer. If he's got an *Entertainment Weekly* magazine or *Variety*, he's a Hollywood "cultural elite" liberal, slumming for the weekend. And if he's got *The Village Voice*, forget it, he's just a nut.

And since *I* didn't have a knapsack, I had just enough time to catch that serene little smile of his before the door shut in my face.

6

ADVENTURES IN POLITICS
1969—1996

MY AMERICAN JOURNEY

I've never really been interested in politics. Which is surprising, I guess, when you consider that as a kid I was witness to one of the most politically-charged eras in American history: the Sixties.

Maybe it was the sight of Mama Cass and Tiny Tim cavorting across my television that accounts for my slightly conservative viewpoints today (it's a wonder they didn't stunt my growth). Even more than that, however, it was scenes like the 1968 Democratic Convention in Chicago that convinced me politics was where adults went when they wanted to act like assholes.

Besides, I was too busy with important things, kid things. I was lucky enough to be 11 when the '69 Mets gave New York one of the greatest sports stories ever. I was at the Garden the night Frazier decisioned Ali. I was old enough to appreciate the significance of the first moon landing, yet still young enough to harbor dreams of doing the same thing myself one day. Who gave a crap about Barry Goldwater?

Even later, to be honest, I didn't really care much about

politics. Maybe it was my upbringing. Elmhurst, Queens, in New York City; according to census figures, the most ethnically diverse neighborhood in the entire United States. People of all sorts, piled on top of each other. We weren't too poor, weren't too rich — strictly working-class, which of course felt right to us, since everyone we knew was also.

Then later there were girls and beer and new wave music and college road trips to Florida in cars that barely made it, and then marriage and work and kids. Politics just didn't seem to matter — they didn't take place in the real world (one look at Senator Paul Simon told me that).

But here's the point. All that time, as soon as I was old enough, I voted. Why? Because while I never cared much for politics, I always knew I was a conservative. And strangely, I remember the exact moment I came to this realization.

My fourth grade teacher was Miss Thibadeau. I've never had a teacher I liked so much. In reality, I was a little in love with her. Okay, more than a little. In retrospect, she was probably all of 23 or so — but to me, naturally, she was the epitome of feminine sophistication and allure.

For a teacher, Miss Thibadeau did kooky, daring things; she dressed however she wanted, including beads and short skirts and knee-high boots; she played the guitar and sang in class, including songs you'd actually heard on the radio *("goodbye, Ruby Tuesday ...")*; sometimes she even decided not to teach, and just gave us a topic and let us "socialize," talking among ourselves in little groups. She was what my father called, none too admiringly, "a little hippie." I thought she was awesome.

Anyway, one day we were excused from morning classes, because the police were coming to our school to give a speech about "the dangers of drugs." I was standing near the back of the auditorium, happy just to be getting out of Math, when somebody tapped my shoulder.

"Who's your teacher?" the principal himself asked me when I turned around.

"Miss Thibadeau, sir," I replied (we always said "sir" in those days — incredible, huh?).

"Do you know where the teachers' room is, on the second floor?" I did. "Would you please go and tell Miss Thibadeau that we need another teacher to keep an eye on things here? Tell her to come down right away, we're about to start."

Big-eyed with mission, I headed out of the auditorium, the Principal's shout of "And don't run!" bouncing unheeded off my back.

If Miss Thibadeau was comely in a classroom, Miss Thibadeau on the telephone in the teachers' lounge was pure heartbreak. She must have been talking to her boyfriend or something, I surmised, as I'd never seen her like this; she was sitting with her bare feet up on the coffee table, giggling and talking in a voice that seemed too young to be hers. For the first time, it actually occurred to me that Miss Thibadeau had a life outside of PS-13.

I was a bit scared, but as she hadn't seen me, I had to get her attention, so I tapped lightly on the open door. When she saw me she gave a little smile, then told whoever she was talking to to hold on, and raised her eyebrows at me — the universal gesture for, "Well?"

"Uh, Miss Thibadeau, Mr. Mondello told me, uh, to tell you to come to the auditorium, um, 'cause they need some more teachers. So he says if you could come down there now."

She rolled her eyes and told the boyfriend or whoever that she had to go. Then she started talking low, so I couldn't hear. I don't know why I waited; I guess I wanted to walk downstairs with her. I swear, I remember my palms were sweating.

Then she said it. The boyfriend must have been annoyed, because she suddenly said, a little louder, "*No*, I have to *go* — the *igspay* are here to give their speech."

My first reaction was to be a little insulted; did she actually think I didn't understand pig-latin? It wasn't until I had followed her downstairs and seated myself in the auditorium, however, watching but not hearing as the cops gave their talk, that I connected it all up.

See, my father was a cop, too. And of course, it being the Sixties, I had heard people call cops "pigs" before, that was no big deal. It was so commonplace, in fact, that I'd heard it used in TV movies; it was the buzz word that immediately identified a made-for-TV radical. But TV — you know, who cared? The cops always won anyway.

But this was Miss Thibadeau. Miss Thibadeau, the beautiful hippie, the flower child who wanted to teach the whole world to sing. *Calling my father a pig*. My father, who coached my basketball team, a team whose group photo looked like a United Nations postcard. My father, who drove all over the neighborhood picking up kids in our battered station wagon to drive them to the games. Who took the team out for ice-cream after practices, or to McDonalds after we lost. Who actually came up to the school himself one time, when I was in first grade, to give a little speech on what it was like to be a cop. I'd never seen him in his uniform before — even I was amazed. And here was this guitar-playing, bead-wearing little hippy calling him a *pig* to some jerk she was dating.

I was shocked. And I was shocked that I was shocked; I hadn't realized my family loyalties ran so deep.

In retrospect, it wasn't even so much that Miss Thibadeau

broke my heart (though of course she did). It was, I think, the fact that she confirmed for me something I already suspected — that she was too good to be true. On some level, I'd already distrusted her. I guess I must have known all along that allowing the class to "socialize" was just an excuse for her to sneak off to the teachers' room for a cigarette.

So while Miss Thibadeau didn't *make* me a conservative, she helped me realize I was one. She helped me realize how basically full of it I would always find people like her. You know. Real "left-wingers." Designer-radicals. *Liberals.*

And let me tell you, this guy Franken? He's Miss Thibadeau with hairy legs. It took a book by a bucktoothed, hairy-legged Miss Thibadeau to remind me of how phony these liberals can be, how pious and inflated, and to make me care about politics for the first time. Care enough to actually write a whole *book* about politics.

That, and of course I'm hoping to make myself a few bucks.

7

WRITER'S BLOCK AND THE PLAGUE OF REVISIONIST HISTORY

Did you ever try to write a whole book? It's like trying to wash an aircraft carrier with a Q-tip.

This was supposed to be a chapter on "revisionist history," and how liberal academia is virtually re-writing American history to conform to their more "enlightened" views. The problem was, I just couldn't figure out where to start. It's such a huge, horrific issue, dismantling it is like tearing down a house — how do you decide what to take apart first?

At this point, I'll admit, I didn't have much of this book done. In fact, I only had some rough notes and an outline. I didn't even have a title; somehow, *Al Franken Is A Big Fat Idiot* didn't quite work, as while I felt it was *almost* right, Franken doesn't look fat. After deliberating awhile, I finally asked myself, "Well, if he's not big and fat, then what is he?" Somehow after that, the title seemed much easier.

But that was as far as I could get. True, I was quite pleased with this title, and happily repeated it to myself often — occasionally bursting into stifled giggles, much to the alarm of my fellow passengers on the southbound "E" train. But otherwise, all I had was a few "bug-eyed-and-ugly" jokes and a burning, insatiable curiosity as to what Jesse Jackson does for a living. As far as substantial, serious issues, I was blank-city.

I began looking for any excuse to avoid writing. I hadn't even managed to finish reading Al's book yet, so I decided it was time to give that a shot. Then I picked it up, and experienced my first pangs of doubt about this whole project. True, it looked like a short book. But that's like the doctor telling you it's only a *little* tumor.

I balanced my checkbook. I alphabetized my CDs. When my oldest came home with homework, I practically leapt out of the chair to help him. Poor kid gave a shriek.

Then a person entered my life who somehow made everything possible, who somehow made it all easy for me. He was so compelling, so inspiring, that I raced for my laptop and began typing, and I never looked back.

It all happened thanks to my son's homework, thanks to Chapter 17 of the Social Studies text, *Our World*. Because that's where I first met the great: Mansa Musa.

8

MANSA MUSA

lright, I know what you're saying: "I don't want to read a whole chapter about Mansa Musa — I learned all about him in grade school." I'm sure you remember. He came right between the lectures on the "intrusive European migrants" and the "despotic John D. Rockefeller." If you *don't* recall the 14th-Century West African King Mansa Musa, shame on you — you must have slept through Liberal History 101.

I included this chapter on revisionist history to show where unchecked liberalism is currently leading academia (also because "Mansa Musa" is a funny name for a chapter). In case you don't remember the brouhaha over revising America's history curriculum, a short synopsis:

In 1989, the National Center for History in the Schools at UCLA (hereinafter "NCH") was put in charge of creating national standards for teaching history. The two directors of this commission of over one hundred history and education experts were Gary Nash and Charlotte Crabtree (who as far as I know bears no relation to the *real* Miss Crabtree, of

Little Rascals fame).

These two spaceshots came up with one hilarious set of recommendations. The scary thing is, they were serious. The guidelines for this new curriculum can be summarized in two basic statements: *include more good stuff* about women, African-Americans, and other minorities, while *avoiding any bad stuff*; and *avoid any good stuff* about white men, while *including more bad stuff*.

After re-reading the recommendations several times, I've concluded that Nash and Crabtree were either playing a mass April Fools gag on the American public, or their stenographer was suffering from mad-cow disease. I'm not going to list them all, but check out a brief smattering of what your kid's curriculum would look like if these educational trailblazers had their way:

• No reference to Paul Revere, Robert E. Lee, Thomas Edison, Alexander Graham Bell, Albert Einstein, the Wright brothers, Jonas Salk, nor to many other minor (white male) historical figures;

• More of a focus on the Klu Klux Klan, the leader of the underground railroad (Harriet Tubman), and "the achievements and grandeur of Mansa Musa's court and the social customs and wealth of the kingdom of Mali" (That's a *quote*. You thought I was joking?);

• No reference to *The Federalist Papers*, but inclusion of the manifesto of the women's suffrage movement, titled the "Declaration of Sentiments";

• More of a focus on the Aztecs and their contributions to "architecture, skills, labor systems and agriculture,"

with no mention of their festive weekend pastime of
cutting out the hearts of living human sacrifices,
generally teenaged female virgins.

In addition to these specific examples, the proposals were
loaded with biased and prejudicial words and phrases. For
instance, the guidelines called for students to analyze
encounters between "intrusive European migrants and
indigenous people." The recommendations also blamed the
United States for the "swordplay" of the Cold War.

The proposals were canned, thank God, after an
independent panel reviewed them and found them as
ridiculous as they sound. Then, in what has to be the first
unanimous vote since pay raises, the Senate passed a
resolution denouncing the proposals (the vote was actually
99-1, but the one vote against the resolution objected
because he demanded a *stronger* condemnation).

Before the recall, however, at least 30,000 copies of this
nonsense were sent out to schools across the country! Some
schools actually began to institute the changes. In one St.
Louis school the reading list now includes a biography of
Anne Morrow Lindbergh, but none for her husband Charles;
and recommends *Sadoko and the Thousand Paper Cranes*,
a story about a child victim of the Hiroshima atomic bomb,
told from the Japanese perspective.

The funniest thing about this reading list, however, is that
these books are intended to teach what the St. Louis school
calls, "history/herstory." *"Herstory?!"* Oh, I get it - *her
story*. That's very clever. I think what we should do now is
ask Mr. Nash and Miss Crabtree to co-chair another panel of
experts to recommend ways to make the English language
completely gender-neutral (I think this time we should
spring for the extra money and hire Spanky and Alfalfa as

well). Let's see, how about Hispanic/Herspanic, Heritage/Hisitage, Antihistamine/Antiherstamine ... well, let's let the experts handle it. That's what they're paid for.

HOW I LEARNED TO START WORRYING AND HATE THE BOMB

While we're on the subject, let me take this moment to direct the revisionist critics of the Hiroshima and Nagasaki attacks to kiss the collective asses of the vets who fought the Japanese during World War II. Remember the revisionist bullshit those bureaucrats wanted to include as part of the *Enola Gay* exhibit at the Smithsonian? "For most Americans, it was a war of vengeance. For most Japanese, it was a war to defend their unique culture against Western Imperialism."

Sounds like a Japanese propaganda film, no? When he realized his precious exhibit was doomed, I'm surprised the author of this garbage didn't sip some saki, bow towards Tokyo, and kamikaze the Smithsonian. Someone needs to remind this history buff that the U.S. was not interested in encroaching on Japan's "unique culture" **until they started dropping fucking bombs on us!** (please re-read last line with Sam Kinison intonation).

And is it really relevant whether the bomb saved a million allied lives or 63,000, which is the number the revisionists

Were The Atomic Bombs Necessary?

Even after the second atomic bomb was dropped, the Japanese Imperial War Council was deadlocked 3 - 3 on whether to surrender or to fight to the end. It was Emperor Hirohito who surprised the group by breaking the deadlock and voting for surrender.

claim? Suddenly 63,000 isn't enough? *We were fighting a war*, and if we saved a hundred allied lives at the expense of our enemy, so be it. Isn't that the point of a

DECEMBER 7, 1941: The Japanese "defending their unique culture against Western imperialism" at Pearl Harbor.

war? To win while incurring as few casualties of your own as possible? Isn't that the way the Spartans set it up?

This is the sort of hand-wringing that turned Vietnam into such a quagmire (whether you were for that war or against it). Look — there's nothing worse than war. Nothing. But with war, you either do it or you don't. Otherwise, it's even worse.

Tell you what — let's put this issue in its proper perspective. Simple question: Do you really think any of these characters moaning about the bomb now would have actually preferred an invasion if *they* had been standing at an airplane hatch with a parachute on, looking down at Tokyo, 1945? Believe me, they would have been sending Oppenheimer candygrams.

And I hope you don't swallow any of this Gar Alperovitz-inspired bullshit that's being thrown around these days — the Japanese were not going to surrender until they were completely broken.* If you don't believe that, talk to a

---

* Gar Alperovitz is not the Latin designation for the Japanese blowfish. He's actually the dean of the A-bomb revisionist school.

witness to the kamikaze attacks or a survivor of a Japanese
P.O.W. camp.** The "Imperial Japanese Army" was
committed, baby. Remember, it took *two* bombs to finally
break them (of course, the war looks slightly different from
the UCLA teacher's lounge fifty years later).

In any case, the director in charge of the Smithsonian
exhibit quit under severe pressure from the American
Legion lobby. The controversial verbiage was erased and, as
a compromise, the exhibit now consists solely of a portion
of the fuselage of the *Enola Gay*. Unfortunately, the
American Legion was unsuccessful in replacing the
controversial wording with their own more classically
profound, "Payback's a Bitch." (Incidentally, I understand
the Nash/Crabtree/McFarland/Switzer commission has
recently recommended the plane be renamed the *Enola Gay
and Lesbian-American*).

WELCOME TO THE UNIVERSITY OF BEVERLY HILLS

I don't know, maybe I'm being too harsh here, maybe
there is something valid about reviewing history from a
modern perspective. Perhaps we *do* need to re-examine

** Yeah, I know they're supposed to be our great trading buddies now, and they're going
to help us keep an eye on China and all that. But Japanese war atrocities remain decidedly
shocking and under-reported. Consider: While the death-rate for Allied POWs in German
camps during WWII was roughly four percent, in Japanese camps it was at least twenty-
seven percent; most of these POWs were killed by medical experiments, malnutrition,
overwork, or simply for fun. Furthermore, Japanese military fanaticism was such that not
only did the kamikaze attacks begin in 1944, when Japan was big-time on the run, but in
some cases they continued *even after the Japanese surrendered*. Japanese kamikaze
techniques, furthermore, were not limited to planes; there were manned torpedoes and
manned rockets, with the doomed pilot steering the bomb to its eventual target.

In the months before Hiroshima, with the tide of war clearly against them, Japanese
leaders exhorted the population to fight to the last man, using spears if necessary. One of
the things which may account for this level of fanaticism is that, among other atrocities
promised, some generals in the Imperial Japanese Army advised the populace that if
Americans were to ever occupy Japan, the invaders would commence eating Japanese
children.

things, to set the record straight, to get to the truth. But do you really think Hollywood should be handling it?

Now I don't know about you, and I'll admit I *had* heard rumblings of it before, but it took Oliver Stone to convince me that the Klingons and Romulans were in on the JFK assassination. And this is a perfect example of why Hollywood should be looked to for guidance in forming our children's historical perspectives.

I mean, before *Panther*, how many of us realized that the F.B.I. and white organized crime conspired to import drugs into the black ghettos in order to wipe out the Black Panther movement? Thanks for clarifying things, Mr. Van Peebles.[+]

And how about Spike Lee's *X*? I didn't realize it had been confirmed that the U.S. Government (read: white) was in cahoots with Louis Farrakhan in planning Malcolm's assassination. I'm glad Professor Lee set the record straight. I'm also glad Spike granted our children a national day of truancy to go see his wonderful film so they could make him even richer.

I guess if nothing else, these movies confirm three members of the original NCH commission.

Now, I realize that history may have become a bit generic and sanitized over the years. Thinking about it, I have no problem teaching all the ugly details of our major historical figures, as long as we tell the whole story. Let's learn everything about Columbus — how he set out to conquer and colonize the new world. Let's teach our children how Thomas Jefferson owned slaves. I think that's fair. Let's take the NCH's advice and ask our children to conduct a trial of

---

[+] I should point out that it hurts me tremendously to criticize Mario Van Peebles. He, of course, co-starred in *Jaws 4 — The Revenge*, one of my all-time favorites. Who can forget the classic scene in which the fifty-foot shark sticks his head out of the water and roars at the camera like Godzilla?

that despotic John D. Rockefeller in which they can accuse him of **"knowingly and willfully participating in unethical and amoral business practices designed to undermine traditions of fair open competition for personal and private aggrandizement in direct violation of the common welfare."** Have a good time, kiddies.

JUST FOR THE RECORD: A BRIEF HISTORY OF MANSA MUSA OF MALI

The founder of the great Malian Empire was Sundiata, who came to the throne in 1307. Sundiata was either the grandfather or granduncle of Mansa Musa. The empire was notable for its incredible wealth in gold, which it gained through a well-orchestrated economic embargo (**"knowingly and willfully participating in unethical and amoral business practices ..."**).

Prior to Mansa Musa's reign, Malian invaders initiated a physical blockade of the gold mines of the ancient Ghanaian Empire. The Malians never seized the gold mines themselves, but because they now controlled the trade routes, the gold was valueless without them (**"... designed to undermine traditions of fair open competition for personal and private aggrandizement ..."**).

Mansa Musa himself gained the throne when his immediate predecessor struck out to cross the Atlantic, looking to expand his empire to new worlds (sound a little like Columbus?). He was never heard from again.

As ruler, Mansa Musa ruled with an iron hand, where to sneeze in his presence meant certain death. Because of his strict policies, crime was almost unheard of, and education and religion flourished like never before in Africa. It is said that children were literally put in chains if they neglected their studies of the Koran.

Mansa Musa, however, is most notable for his historic

journey to Mecca in 1324. Musa lead a caravan of at least 60,000 men, including his personal retinue of 12,000 *slaves* (sound a little like Jefferson?) across the desert to the holy city. Once in Mecca, Musa distributed so much gold that he depressed the gold market for the next 12 years (**"... in direct violation of the common welfare."**). Mansa Musa died in 1332.

(So now that we've covered that, how about giving George Washington a little equal time, huh? I mean, he may not have been perfect — but at least you could sneeze around him).

9

CAMP BLEEDING HEART

You remember that kid who was always picked last when you were choosing up sides in grade school? Or how about that obnoxious kid who wrote for the school paper and was always trying to contradict the teacher? The one who stuck to his dorm room in college, not going to any of the parties or events, who wasn't very friendly and who nobody ever knew or really cared to know? Remember how sometimes you would feel bad for these characters?

Well guess what? You needn't have bothered — they were just biding their time. Because every year, a bunch of them collects for one of America's most exclusive, high-powered get-togethers. And this time, we're the ones not invited.

In his book, Franken breathlessly gives us the details of some quality time he gets to spend with none other than Bill Clinton himself. And where could such an incongruous pair possibly meet, you ask? Why, at Renaissance Weekend, of course.

What? You never heard of Renaissance Weekend?

Lucky soul. Because the only way you would know about Renaissance Weekend is if you were a member in good standing of the elite liberal clique that participates in this incestuous charade every year (that, or if you had read Al's book, an experience much like having your wisdom teeth extracted with a butter knife). But since I had to read Al's book in order to write this one, and since I had to research Renaissance Weekend, I'll fill you in on this secret little left-wing day camp.

In his book, Franken describes Renaissance Weekend as a four-day affair of "off the record exchanges of ideas 'in the Renaissance spirit.'" Organized by an old Harvard buddy of Franken's (which explains Al's invitation), it's held on Hilton Head Island off South Carolina, and is supposed to bring together "people of achievement" from various walks of life (at least those "people of achievement" who can afford the $1500 per couple fee).

Apparently, few of America's prominent conservatives are "achievers," because Al himself describes the event as "predominantly liberal, with a few token right-wingers." I guess I missed something back in high school, because I just have to ask: That's the Renaissance spirit?! Gathering together as many people as you can who feel exactly the same way on virtually every issue?

Free exchange of ideas, my ass. This is a chance for all these liberal yahoos to tell each other how wonderful they are while they sip iced cappuccino and swap Newt Gingrich haircut jokes. Can you imagine the chat that must go on at this thing during the big Saturday cookout?

Hillary (waggling a finger significantly): ... and so that's why, *philosophically-speaking*, conservatism *is* fascism.

Franken: Brilliantly put!

Stephanopoulos: How true!

Tipper: I couldn't agree more! Say something funny, Al.

What fun! Soy-burgers and not-dogs, all around!

Apparently, one of the highlights of the big weekend is a touch football game in which President Clinton himself participates. Frankly, I'd pay to see this, as this gang of editors, politicos, and all-around spazzes on a playing field of any sort must look like the basketball scene from *One Flew Over the Cuckoo's Nest.* Franken gives this description of the proceedings: "The young, Kennedyesque President-elect frolicking with windswept Renaissancers ..." *Horf.* I suspect Al would sound a bit less enraptured if the Chief Executive Load happened to fall on him.

Anyway, spurred by Franken's rhapsodizing on this event, I went and dug up a few reports about the shadowy goings-on at Renaissance Weekend, and about the various "profound" discussions and activities. When I eventually stopped laughing, I realized that the situation here is exactly as it appears. The real story is not the President's wheezing attempt at being an every-day-kind-of-guy by lurching around a football field. Nor is it the fact that Wolf Blitzer kept trying to dribble the football during the big game.

No, the real story is that the Democrats who gathered on Hilton Head Island were galvanized by the idea that the weekend is some sort of profound intellectual excercise, while simultaneously not appreciating the fact that the nearest dissenting voice could only be reached by boat. This is the "common touch" Democrats, huh?

Why did they bother? They could have handled this whole thing by phone. My suggestion would be that next year, they just call and leave each other voice mails saying, "You know what? I agree with you! Bye!" At least then nobody has to see Jeff Greenfield in a bathing suit.

RENAISSANCE WEEKEND — ROSTER OF EVENTS

7:30am- Wake up call. President leads group jog around lake. Oxygen and CPR available.

7:33am- Breakfast in main chow room. Moments of silence strictly prohibited!

9:30am- Good Morning Lecture & Exercise: "American Complicity in Bosnian Genocide" and low-impact step-class.

12:00pm-Lunch. Macrobiotic picnic on the Green.

1:00pm- Workshop: The under-appreciated craft of Vietnamese scrimshaw.

2:00pm- Afternoon Lecture: "Confucius — Sage, Poet, African." Dr. Leonard Jeffries, CCNY.

3:00pm- Sensitivity Training. All straight
white males of European ancestry
must attend.

4:00pm- Coordinated stress-relief communal-
bonding activity: Bobbing for tofu.

5:00pm- Dinner. Come join us for a vegan
feast!

6:00pm- Panel Discussion: "America's
Military: Necessary?"

6:30pm- Documentary film screening: "The
Common Housefly — Species On The
Brink."

7:30pm- Evening Lecture: "Homoeroticism in
Ye Olde Farmer's Almanac."

8:00pm- Play: "What to Do When You
Discover Your Significant Other is
Another's Other (When the Rainbow
is Enuf)."

10:00pm-Bonfire on the badminton court:
Come join us for a traditional Mayan
chant-along around the fire.

11:00pm-Ceremonial flag-lowering, main quad.

11:05pm-Ceremonial flag-burning, main quad.

10

AL FRANKEN IS A SMUG LITTLE HYPOCRITE

Rush Limbaugh is a Big Fat Idiot and Other Observations

By Al Franken
271 pp. Delacorte Press:
$21.95

o far, 1996 is turning out to be the year of the political bestseller. We've had all sorts of political books doing well. As a relatively recent convert to political activism, I think this is great — people are reading, they're concerned. It's certainly better than getting your politics from a Sting album or an episode of *Sally Jessy Raphael.*

But since there seems to be a predominance of liberal books coming out so far this season (that could change, of course), I thought I'd review a few of these "notes from the left" in my own book. And let's face it, where to start is pretty obvious.

Now, I think it's a reasonably safe assumption that most of you reading this have probably not read Franken's book, and have no desire to. So I'll make a deal with you. In return for your having bought this book, I'll give you a few quick lowlights from Al's manifesto. That way, when you tell people you can't stand Al Franken, and they ask you why, you'll have an answer beyond, "Because I actually paid to see that *Stuart Smalley* movie." *

IF AN INFINITE NUMBER OF LIBERALS WERE GIVEN AN INFINITE NUMBER OF LAPTOPS ...

Now as you've probably gathered, I didn't enjoy Al's book. But to be honest, that's not because of his politics (well, maybe a little). No, the thing that makes reading Al's book about as pleasant as an IRS audit is his absolute *smugness*. Nobody this year — not even Bob Woodward — has produced a book as transparently self-serving as has Franken (well, maybe Hillary — but one bullshit artist at a time).

You see, it's just so clear that writing *Rush Limbaugh is a Big Fat Idiot* was Franken's attempt to set himself up in business as the left's official humorist (this because the last successful joke he's written was performed by John Belushi). For that reason, Al spends as much time kissing liberal ass as he does trying to be funny. You wouldn't believe how obsequious this guy can get — he's like a left-

---

* For the uninitiated among you, Stuart Smalley is a character Al has played on *Saturday Night Live* and, recently, in a movie. The character, a simpering basket case addicted to 12-step programs, is apparently based in part on Franken's own experiences in the recovery culture. Stuart's motto is, "I'm good enough, I'm smart enough, and doggone it, people like me." (The possibilities for wisecracks here are so profound, I think I'll just leave it to you. Just make sure you show no mercy — this Stuart character is almost as annoying as Al is).

Tell you what, let me get you started: *Stuart Smalley may be a pathetic whimpering _____, but he makes Al Franken look like _____.*

See? Wasn't that fun? Alright, don't get a swelled head. Let's remember who's supposed to be the writer here.

wing Igor. This tactic has apparently worked so well for
Franken, he's managed to gain access to political events he
normally wouldn't see without a waiter's uniform. And at
these events, like an organ-grinder's monkey, Al performs
right on cue.

For instance, Franken delights in describing how he
corners people like Newt Gingrich and Al D'Amato at
political functions, and then is purposely rude to their faces,
as if normal human courtesy is somehow beneath a great
liberal satirist. Franken goes off on a holier-than-thou jag
when he confronts Gingrich over the economy, despite the
fact that Gingrich is clearly not interested in Franken's
opinions. He then rushes at Al D'Amato in order to tell the
Senator a particularly lame joke referring to D'Amato's
recent heart trouble.

Franken does this sort of thing so incessantly, the reader
eventually begins to wonder: What is this compulsion Al has
to be totally rude to any conservative he meets? Is he hoping someone just clocks him, so he can sue and get his teeth
fixed? Doesn't he realize that by talking to him, these people
are only being courteous, and they really just want him to
shut up and go away? (Of course, that charming voice of
Al's doesn't help his case. A more curdling, adenoidal drone
you're not likely to find this side of Arnold Horshack. But at
least Horshak hasn't attempted a comeback).** You would
think Al had outgrown this sort of name-calling by now;
after all, the Sixties were a long time ago, the "Revolution"

** Wrong I am. Thanks to my editor's mysterious devotion to Ellen DeGeneres, it's been
pointed out to me that Horshack is indeed back. Ron Palillo, the actor who played
Horshack, has emerged from a 10-year bout with agoraphobia to land a role on the hit TV
show *Ellen*. Was it Ronald Reagan that sent both Palillo and Franken into exile during the
Eighties? Did honking, bushy-haired, psuedo-comedians have a thing about Ron? And
what mysterious shift in the solar winds accounts for the return of these two figures?
Who's next? Gary MuleDeer?

is long over.

Another part of Al's crusade is to point out the "intellectual dishonesty" of the G.O.P. But Franken's own book is about as "intellectually honest" as a Stalin-era *Pravda*. For instance:

• At one point Franken praises Bill Clinton's "don't end it, mend it," approach to affirmative action, as if Clinton has solved this issue once and for all. Al even uses this as his point of departure for telling us how Clinton is "the greatest President of the twentieth century." Only problem is, Franken never tells us exactly *how* Clinton plans to "mend it." And that's because Clinton doesn't plan to "mend" anything. Clinton, in fact, hasn't done a *single thing* on affirmative action all term, other than talk about it. "Mend it, don't end it"? Spare me the rhymes, Al — I wasn't a member of the Simpson jury.

• Speaking of L.A.'s favorite murderer, Al brings O.J. up at one point. See, Franken is constantly setting himself up as some sort of moral barometer, based on nothing more than his leftist pedigree. And so he tells us that he "didn't follow the O.J. Simpson trial" but that he "will say this about O.J. The man has suffered enough." Gee, I guess those of us on the right have been persecuting O.J. We really have been out of line in making that poor man suffer through a trial. I'm so ashamed.

Let me get this straight. O.J. Simpson has "suffered enough"? That guilty bastard practically cut his wife's head off! Besides, if Franken didn't even "follow the trial," how the hell can he know if O.J. has "suffered enough"? How can he have any opinion on Simpson's guilt or innocence?

• Franken actually has the gall to write, "I'm making fun of meanness in public debate by being mean myself. It's called 'irony.' Perhaps you've heard of it?" Al, if you're going to attack guys like Reagan and Dole on a personal level, at least have the God-given balls to own up to it! And if you think your blatantly obnoxious book is "ironic," you better buy yourself a dictionary. Then you can also look up "sanctimonious." Perhaps you've heard of it?

The book is full of this sort of self-promoting nonsense — the guy doesn't let up. He reprints positive reviews of his work at least five or six times ("the man responsible for some of the most brilliant political satire of our time ..."); he congratulates himself on his political acumen ("Not Dan Rather, not Tom Brokaw, not Peter Jennings ... none of them understood what I understood"); and he name-drops like a PR man trying to get laid. And all just to make sure somebody saves him a seat at the next White House Correspondents Dinner.

See, that's what I meant when I said that it wasn't so much his politics, but his smugness, the advertisements for himself, that make Franken's book so "enjoyable" (now *that's* irony. See the difference?).

In any event, after reading Franken's book I decided I had to find out more about the left's new point man. I mean, what kind of a guy writes a "political work" that spends half its time telling us how wonderful its author is? If I was going to write my book, I had to get to the heart of this new Jonathan Swift. And that search eventually led me to the mysterious ... Deep Throat.

11

ADVENTURES IN POLITICS
JUNE 7, 1996

MY VERY OWN "DEEP THROAT"

My quest to discover the real Al Franken, to find out what makes this political maverick tick, led me down many dead-ends. My first move was to read the *Saturday Night Live* books, the memoirs, all loaded with accounts of Al's combative behavior on the show, where he was about as popular backstage as a heckler with a megaphone. Yeah, I covered all those quickly enough. But those are books, you know? Second-hand accounts. I wanted insight. I wanted a *source*.

I decided I had to pound the pavement, to unearth someone who could somehow help me understand just what makes the "greatest comic mind of the twentieth century" run as it does. So I searched the SNL books for clues. I followed up tips. And after phone calls, negotiations, and dogged investigatory work that dominated nearly an entire lunch hour, I found that source. My very own Deep Throat.

The following excerpts are from an interview which took

place between myself and a former associate of Al
Franken's. The meeting took place in the shadowy depths of
a saloon on New York's upper East Side, an establishment
which must remain nameless (Kinsale Tavern). All I can
reveal is that Deep Throat is a man who has known Al
Franken as well as it is possible to know this enigmatic
genius.

J.P.: You were with Al Franken from high school?

Deep: Uh-huh.

J.P.: Then you went to California?

Deep: Well, Franken went to Harvard, graduated in '73. In
'73 I moved to Harvard, in order to go down to New York
on the weekends to play at the Improv. And this is at a time
when there was Freddie Prinze, Gabe Kaplan, J.J. Walker ...
Then we moved to L.A., lived there for two years. Basically,
we had no money, but we were both single, at that time, and
there was lots of drugs and girls and basketball ... we had no
money, but we had so much fun, I just can't tell you. And
then we got the job at *Saturday Night Live*. We moved from
L.A. to New York in July of '75.

J.P.: Any stories about you and Al, from before SNL?

Deep: Oh, yes, yes. There's all these stories of being on the
road and doing colleges and chasing girls and doing drugs
and driving through tornadoes ... We just had so much fun. I
know that he has wonderful memories, as I do, of those
years. We had some wild times ... And see, we always had
our act. And we had an agent. We were doing a lot of

colleges, but we couldn't get into the cast of *Saturday Night Live*.

J.P.: You had been trying?

Deep: Al is still trying.

J.P.: Tell me about Al back then. He looks like the sort of guy who, back in high school, had the "kick me" sign on his back. Is that accurate?

Deep: Ah, he was doing the kicking. That's why I picked him to be on my team. I didn't want to work against him. And he finally turned on me. He's a bit of a bully.

J.P.: He is —

Deep: Yeah, he's a bully.

J.P.: As I understand it, on the show in its beginning stages, there was a lot of smoking and drinking, including Franken.

Deep: Oh, there was so many drugs. Yeah, frankly, that's what you get for sharing. He never paid for it, he just did everyone else's drugs. And then told everybody they were drug addicts, after he did their drugs.

J.P.: Is that right?

Deep: Yeah! How about that? Of course, I no longer do drugs like that, nobody does. I'm not here suggesting that it's a good idea.

J.P.: About the break-up. Was it purely financial or was it personal or ...

Deep: Oh, Franken always insisted that he was the guy who did the business ... So instead of arguing, I let him do it. As it turns out, he was as bad a businessman as I was. But he wouldn't admit it. That's my complaint with Franken, that he has a pathological inability to admit mistakes.

J.P.: He's egotistical?

Dav — Ooops, I mean **Deep**: Yes, but so am I. Who is not egotistical who is in show business? You have to be.

J.P.: And alcohol and drugs figured in?

Deep: Yes ... He didn't approve, and so our partnership broke up. About smoking and drinking. That was it. That's where he decided that my opinion was not as worthy as his ... my work wasn't as good as his.

J.P.: Right around the time you guys broke up, is when he discovered Stuart Smalley ...

Deep: Yes.

J.P.: You were replaced by Stuart Smalley.

Deep: Yes. He was in Al Anon ... He got the new religion, and wanted me to bow down before that God too. And I didn't want to. And I was resented.

J.P.: He became sanctimonious?

Deep: He certainly was. He was sanctimonious.

J.P.: He won't work with you because you drink?

Deep: That's right. And it used to be part of our act! It was fun. There was nothing pathetic about it. Then all of a sudden, he changed, and it wasn't funny anymore.... That was the end of *Franken and* ——. He no longer looked at me or talked to me the same way. He no longer valued my opinion. He doesn't need me, he doesn't want me around ... I knew I was in trouble in 1980 when Al said, "Do you wanna help me write the 'Al Franken Decade' movie?"

J.P.: Wow.

Deep: And I went, "well, wait a minute, no I don't want to write the 'Al Franken Decade' movie. I want to write the *'Franken and* ——*'* movie." That was 1980. So I did have a glimpse of the future there.

J.P.: Now, it seems that when it comes to Bill Clinton, Al is a real suck —

Deep: Oh, anybody more powerful than Al, he's a real suck ass! Anybody who works below him, he shits on. A lot of the people on the show who disliked him were all underneath him. All the people who liked him were above him.

J.P.: Is that why he was not liked on *Saturday Night Live*?

Deep: Yes.

J.P.: As I understand it, he's no longer writing for *Saturday Night Live*.

Deep: No. I hope he got fired.

The "Al Franken Decade" movie?

What's interesting here is that, as of this writing, the Clinton Administration is scrambling to distance itself from anyone with a history of drug use (this due to allegations made by Gary Aldrich, a 30-year FBI agent who worked in White House security).

So while Stephanopoulos desperately assures us that people with a history of significant drug use would not be tolerated by the White House, Bill Clinton and Al Franken continue to schmooze together along the campaign trail. The President has now even taken to chauffeuring "Stuart Smalley" around town. Here's a quote from the July 1, 1996 edition of *The New York Post*:

> Comedian Al Franken is still laughing about the limo ride he shared with President Clinton after a New York fund-raiser last week. It seems that the Prez' briefcase slipped off the limo's seat — spilling his credit cards on the floor. Picking them up, Franken winked, "I could have stolen one of these." "Yeah, you could have," drawled the President. "But you probably wouldn't have a big line of credit."

Which proves, if nothing else, that Mr. Clinton has poor judgment when it comes to picking friends.

(Alright, I guess my Deep Throat is not all that mysterious. But at least he has a better memory than Craig

Livingstone.

Tom Davis, who worked as Al Franken's comedy partner for over 16 years, is currently hosting, "Trailer Park," a very funny show on The Science Fiction Channel. In addition, he somehow finds time to devote to several film and writing projects of his own).

12

TIPPER, THEY SHRUNK THE PENIS!
AL GORE AND THE ENVIRONMENT

he job of Vice-President of the United States is an interesting gig. While occasionally he gives a speech to the graduates or to the Paramus Rotary Club or something, let's face it; most of the time the Vice President is just hanging around waiting for the President to die. He gets up every morning, calls his office; if they tell him the President is still breathing, he goes back to bed. Vice-President is essentially America's longest-running no-show job.

Al Gore is uniquely suited to this. Al is the kind of guy who could roller-skate down the street with his head on fire and people wouldn't notice. Not many people have this ability to blend into the background undetected; but Al's a born coat-holder. Quick — when was the last time you saw him? See what I mean?

There is, however, one point in time when the Vice

President does have a purpose above simply occupying the executive on-deck circle. And that is — election time.

"OUR BOGUS FUTURE"

Remember Al Gore's moniker during the '92 campaign — "Mr. Ozone?" Neither do I. And you know why? Because we haven't heard it *since* 1992. Since the '92 campaign, neither Gore nor anyone else in the Clinton administration has been on the tree stump over the environment. But now that Election '96 has rolled around, it looks like the Clinton team has finally found something for Al to do.

You see, some polls conducted in late 1995 indicated that during the '96 election the Republicans might be vulnerable on their environmental agenda. Which means the Clinton people decided it was time to turn Al Gore, White House lawn ornament into ... *Al Gore, Greenpeace Warrior!*

How exactly were they going to accomplish this? Well, last time he wrote a book. Hmmm, if it worked once ...

Al's instant passion for the environment has this time shown up in a book he describes as "critically important." Published to much fanfare in March of 1996, the book is titled *Our Stolen Future*, and Gore wrote the introduction. In it he asserts, among other things, that studies have linked synthetic chemicals in our environment to "infertility; genital deformities; hormonally triggered human cancers such as those of the breast and prostate gland; neurological disorders in children; and developmental and reproductive problems in wildlife" (Al only gives us an intro this time around, not a whole book — he's been busy honing his ukelele chops).

The book itself goes on to build a case for excessive chemicals in our environment being the cause of everything from falling human sperm counts to lesbian sea gulls to the shrinking size of alligator penises. Scary stuff, huh? There's only one problem with it.

It's complete bullshit.

According to Niels Skakkebaek, the *very scientist* whose work is cited as the foundation for *Our Stolen Future*, "It is premature to call for a ban on these or any other chemicals before more research is done. They (environmentalists) are misrepresenting this research."

Widespread testing has in fact shown that the book's conclusions are utterly groundless. Even the National Academy of Sciences has concluded that, on the cancer issue, levels of synthetic carcinogens are "so low that they are unlikely to pose an appreciable cancer risk." One prominent researcher sums it all up this way: "Something is missing in *Our Stolen Future* and that's called science."

Overall, the consensus in the scientific community is that the book is "very unscientific," and that when it comes to the environment, Al Gore should just stick to pressing leaves in his big red dictionary.

The whole project was suspect from the get-go. Even the *author of the book* has been quoted as telling a convention of environmental supporters, "I've become even more crafty about finding the voices to say the things I think are true. That's my subversive mission." Meanwhile, the PR firm handling the book turns out to be the same bunch responsible for the Alar scare a few years back, another alarm that was later discredited.

It's at this point that I began to think maybe synthetic chemicals have damaged Al Gore's cerebral cortex. For crying out loud Al, didn't the Alar thing set off a few bells? How could you so whole-heartedly endorse a book that was about to scare half the world to death before at least making sure the science checked out? I mean — it's a jerkoff gig and all, but this guy *is* the Vice President. A lot of people are going to listen to him. The ones with an extra chromosome, anyway.*

I guess Al just felt that, this being an election year, he better do something "green" — and fast. And that's because of the wonderful track record his administration has accumulated since the last time Al climbed into bed with Mother Nature.

GORE AGONISTES

A Bush-era quote from Al Gore: "The ecological system that supports life as we know it is ... in imminent and grave danger. And yet the pattern of our politics remains unchanged."

And a quote from 1993, while setting up a new White House department: "This new Office on Environmental Policy is a major step forward ... it's a new approach to the environment." Well, let's take a look at how sincere the administration's "new approach" has been, shall we?

The Clinton administration's biggest act of environmental sincerity has to be approving the bill which allowed for 4.5 billion feet of salvage logging in ancient forest groves on federal lands. President Clinton is so proud of this act that he now says he "regrets" signing that bill, and that he actually didn't mean to do it (I guess his hand slipped).

We can also credit the administration with signing the legislation addressing the "unfunded mandates" issue. This

---

* Yeah, I know that's a rather cruel and tasteless joke. But I couldn't resist tossing that back at Al. Al Gore on Oliver North's 1994 Senate campaign: "He is banking on the fact that he can raise enough money from the extreme right wing, the extra chromosome right wing, to come in and buy enough advertising to just overwhelm the truth."

sounds complicated, but it's not. It essentially declared that market forces, not government regulations, would now govern how environmental issues are dealt with; this took much of the control away from the feds, and gave it to big industries. Which is like putting Michael Jackson in charge of a kindergarten.

Let's see, what else? For the first time in 15 years, the importation of PCBs (nasty stuff that causes cancer, liver damage, and other holiday favorites) is back. Estimates say thousands of people will eventually die due to PCB-laced fish in the Great Lakes region alone (guess that region must vote Republican).

And just to round out the field, how about the administration throwing in the towel on the fuel efficiency issue, and their assuring agricultural producers continued use of methyl bromide, the toxin eating at the ozone layer.

The bottom line here is that the Clinton administration's record on the environment stinks like Love Canal at low tide — and *that's* why we haven't heard from Mr. Ozone since 1992.

Realistically though, the issue with this is not so much the environment, which is always a subject of great debate. No, the issue is *accountability*. Clearly, Al's obsession with the environment runs in cycles four years apart. Why didn't somebody bring all this up last Earth Day?

But now that it's an issue again for the Democrats in '96, no doubt we'll soon be hearing about how Al Gore actually *wrote a book* on the environment. And when will Al and Tipper start communing with nature again during their "casual" after-dinner walks in the park, replete with full camera crew? Yes, from now 'til November, expect to see a lot of the *impassioned* version of Al Gore.

Try to contain your elation.

13
POP QUIZ:
KNOW YOUR LIBERAL
JOURNALISTS!

urprise! Time for a pop quiz to see if you've been paying attention. Now, 1996 is an election year. And that being the case, it is once again time to brace ourselves for an onslaught of liberal "coverage" dished out by those talking haircuts of the journalism game — the anchormen. Generally speaking, anchormen are to real journalists what golfers are to real athletes, but hey, at least they can afford cosmetic surgery.

Anyway, it's important to know exactly who it is that's talking down to you on the four major news networks. So after much research, I put together this exhaustive quiz covering everything you need to know to be a discriminating viewer/voter for Election '96. Take the quiz as many times as you need in order to achieve a perfect score, and if necessary, memorize the correct answers until you know them by heart. Then when you're done, vote Republican.

1. Which of the following network news anchors, born in South Dakota, was a high school pole-vaulter (probably in an effort to get out of South Dakota)? Hint: His industry nickname is "Duncan the Wonderhorse."

a. Benjamin Disraeli
b. Bella Abzug
c. Gene Rayburn
d. Tom Brokaw *(Duncan the Wonderhorse?)*

2. Which network news anchor actually gushed the following lines after O.J. fled the cops in his white Bronco? *"Perhaps O.J. Simpson was trying to do what he does better than anyone else. To run — and by running, to make his dream come true."*

a. Jeff Gillooly
b. Andrea Dworkin
c. Jackie Chan
d. Dan Rather *(Good lord — what's your frequency, Dan?)*

3. Which great American network news anchor refused to become a U.S. citizen until 1994, and enjoys the industry nickname, "Stanley Stunning"? (barf)

a. Dick York
b. Dick Sargent
c. Toru Tanaka
d. Peter Jennings *(The only stunning thing about this guy is that he actually dated Streisand).*

4. Which White House correspondent is such a spokesman for the Clinton Administration that fellow Washington reporters refer to his network as the "Clinton News Network"?

a. Willie Stargell
b. Richard Berendzen
c. Wavy Gravy
d. Wolf Blitzer *(Yes, not technically an anchorman, but has a funny name and looks like Eddie Munster's doll).*

Answers:
1. d
2. d
3. d
4. a (Just kidding — but if you actually had to look at these answers, you *might* have believed that Willie Stargell is working for CNN).

14

New From Dreamworks, It's ...
THE AMERICAN PRESIDENCY

starring **Bill Clinton**

with **Hillary Rodham Clinton**
as his long-suffering wife

Al Gore
as Vice President and White House hat-rack

cameo appearance by **Al Franken** *as "The Fool"*

Soundtrack by **Roger Clinton**

Short-Run Engagement!

ith the big election coming up, I can't help wondering what Clinton's Hollywood connections will mean to him this time around. Is the love affair still in bloom?

Remember 1992's cast of supporting players? Norman Lear, Barbra Streisand, Steven Spielberg, David Geffen, to name just a few. Remember that crack from Peter Guber? "This is the first time a President is younger than Mick Jagger. Hollywood wants to be a part of this inauguration, to claim it." They wanted to *claim* Bill Clinton's inauguration? Hey Peter, you can have it.

The thing that perplexed me at the time, and *really* has

me wondering now, is: Why? What the hell is Hollywood's interest in making sure Bill Clinton is President?

I mean, their support in '92 was no meager effort. In fact, with the exception of the financial community, the entertainment industry was Clinton's biggest supporter. During the election season, the entertainment industry (i.e. Hollywood) donated more than $2.6 million to the Democratic National Committee. Uber-liberals David Geffen, Jeffrey Katzenberg, and Lew Wasserman alone contributed more than $500,000.

And remember that quote from singing nose Barbra Streisand? "If George Bush is elected President, I'm moving to Canada." (If George Bush had been elected President, I would have bought her the ticket — in fact, I'll buy her the ticket anyway). And what about TV producers Harry and Linda Bloodworth-Thomason? When not devising new ways to insult America with shows like *Evening Shade* and *Hearts Afire*, they were busy as Clinton's media consultants, and later choreographed his inauguration.

I guess at the time I just assumed all these hotshots were trying to cozy up to the candidate who would vote their way on issues impacting their industry. But now I'm not so sure. Because best I can tell, since '92 there's been only two issues raised that have affected Hollywood — and Clinton has screwed them both times.

First there was the issue of France and American movies. The French declared that certain cultural items were no longer subject to free trade, giving them the right to control imports of certain goods, including American films. The new rule actually targeted American movies, and essentially boiled down to a quota. Hollywood execs practically choked on their granola.

Now, we all know that the French are not exactly

renowned for their backbone (see "France Bends Over For Hitler," *The New York Times*, June 23, 1940). And I think it's obvious that Clinton held enough foreign policy cards to "gently persuade" those Gallic prangs to "review" this new policy. But he didn't.

Then, of course, there was the V-chip. That's this new device that can be put into TV sets that allows parents to monitor the shows their kids watch. It works off a ratings system similar to the movie industry's. The 1996 Telecommunications Act calls for the installation of V-chips into television sets within two years, and warned the television industry that if they didn't come up with the ratings system to be used with the V-chip, Washington would do it for them. Of course, Hollywood viewed this as a form of censorship, and opposed it vehemently. Clinton signed the bill anyhow. (Incidentally, Canada is introducing the V-chip in September of 1996. I wonder if Streisand knows this? Please, nobody tell her). By all accounts, these are the only two Presidential issues that have had a direct impact on Hollywood in the last four years, and both have gone against La La land.

So where does this leave the relationship between Hollywood and Bill Clinton? Well, logic dictates Hollywood should now have no faith in him, should ignore the coming election, and should return to grooming the next Yahoo Serious. Strangely, however, this seems not to be the case.

At first Hollywood *did* appear to be somewhat disillusioned with Clinton (apparently, they realized the cream puff Slick Willy promised was a station car at best). But guess what? Once the Republicans managed to take over Congress in 1994, Clinton's Hollywood supporters quickly decided to end their little temper tantrum. And early indications seem to suggest contributions from Hollywood this election season will be just as high as in '92.

David Geffen, for instance, has already hosted a $2 million fund-raiser for Clinton in April '95, and is expected to do it again in '96; Spielberg and Katzenberg (the other 2/3 of the mega-company *Dreamworks*) gave the Democratic Party $100,000 each in '95, and will probably do it again in '96; Streisand has already donated $61,000; and through fund-raising, Tom Hanks has helped funnel over a million dollars to the effort.

So what's their angle? Now that it's clear they're not courting his vote on these entertainment issues, I'm completely confused. Why do these people spend their money, not to mention their highly valuable time, backing Clinton? For some, like Linda Ronstadt and Dweezil Zappa, it's obviously just an attempt to get their name in the paper (any paper). And Streisand's probably just looking for a date. But what about all these other stars? What's their motivation?

You can forget about any patriotic angle. Those Hollywood egos don't give a shit about anything that's not going to put their names up in lights. So the idea that they're just interested in involving themselves in the democratic process of a Presidential election goes right out the window.

Are they bored? I don't think so. Excluding Henry Winkler, there are some pretty busy folks on the support list: Robert DeNiro, Richard Dreyfuss, Melanie Griffith, etc.

Are they afraid of another Blacklist scare? Nah, that was 40 years ago, and Communism is long dead, no thanks to them (see next chapter).

No, the best I can figure it, it's got to be just a power thing. The only group or industry on this planet that may wield power comparable to these Hollywood names is found in Washington. These Hollywood fat-cats want to be able to talk to the President on the phone ... that's power. They want a ride on Air Force-One ... that's power. They want to snort coke in the Lincoln bathroom ... that's power. And once you've got fame and money, power is all that's left.

Now don't misunderstand me here, they're not gaining any *real* power. Clinton's voting record makes that perfectly clear. They're gaining that "I did brunch with Stephanopoulos" sort of power. You know, that "Well next time I see Hillary, I'll ask her" sort of power. It's the invitation to the inauguration, the photo shoot with the President, *the appearance* of power, the image.

And of course, Hollywood can't wait to return the favor. As soon as Bill is no longer in power, you can bet that rolodexes all over LA will suddenly be one card lighter. Can you see Clinton trying to get Steven Spielberg to return his calls? "But ma'am, this is the eighth time I've called ... I used to be the *President* ma'am!"

"Yes sir, I'm sure you and Mr. Spielberg are *very* good friends. But I'm afraid he's getting measured for arch supports just now ..."

So my opinion? Look for Hollywood's glitz all over Election '96. And when it's all over, with any luck, Streisand's next album will be "Live From the Yukon."

15

JEANE KIRKPATRICK: KEEPING LIBERALS AWAKE NIGHTS

'll admit that when I read Chapter One of Franken's book, I thought it was for real, and I thought it was hilarious. I kept thinking, "How did the *Times* get Kirkpatrick to review this silly little book?"

See, Franken's opening chapter, titled "Book Review," contains what I later deduced was a mock review of his book by former United Nations ambassador and Reagan foreign policy advisor, Jeane Kirkpatrick. Following the mock review is a mock response from Franken, in which he claims, among other things, to have had an affair with the now 69-year-old Kirkpatrick (potentially the most distasteful coupling since Roseanne's last honeymoon). When I realized that the whole thing was a joke, I realized something else: it wasn't funny anymore. The thing that made the bit funny was the idea that the very serious Kirkpatrick actually read Franken's allegations of their love affair.

But another thing struck me when I realized it was a joke: Why Kirkpatrick? She hasn't held political office in years.* Why pick her for this mock piece? The answer, I then realized, is that Kirkpatrick has been a thorn in the side of liberals since she fled the Democratic Party and turned Republican in the mid-1980s.

You know why? Because besides rising to the highest rank a woman has ever held in U.S. foreign policy, and doing it as a Republican, Dr. Kirkpatrick, in her role as Reagan foreign-policy advisor, is responsible for devising the plan that hugely facilitated the destruction of the left's forty-year pet doctrine: Communism. Rarely has history vindicated one side of such a huge debate so clearly. The conservatives won and the liberals lost, and to quote the eminent Dr. Bunker, "case closed."

But the liberal doves still won't admit defeat. Their response to why communism fell? Listen to this quote, from Deputy Secretary of State, Strobe Talbott: "A new consensus is emerging, that the Soviet threat is not what it used to be. The real point, however, is that it never was. The doves in the Great Debate of the past 40 years were right all along."

Oh, *I* get it, Strobe (Strobe?). The liberals are right because the conservatives *won*. We're supposed to believe that the only reason we managed to outlast communism was because it was never a threat to anyone to begin with (except Afghanistan, perhaps) (and Hungary) (and Czechoslovakia) (and Poland).

---

* This doesn't mean she has disappearred, however. Dr. K is currently co-chair of the Dole campaign and a member of Dole's foreign policy "Dream Team" that also includes George Bush and Henry Kissinger. One look at this lineup and expect China and North Korea to start donating to the Clinton campaign big-time.

I bet even the liberals are embarrassed by this feeble bootstrapping argument (then again, if they're not embarrassed by Sam Donaldson's hairpiece ...). They would probably rather talk about Cuba, and how Castro is still going strong. "Hey, have you heard about the wonderful new social programs Fidel has instituted? Free condoms for prostitutes under ten and a chicken in every living room."

I guess someday soon the Democrats will tell us, "Hey, the Republicans didn't kill affirmative action. We always said it was weak and going to die out anyway."

You know what? I could live with that.

16
CARVILLE VS. FRANKEN

**We're Right, They're Wrong
— A Handbook For
Spirited Progressives**
By James Carville
183 pp. Random House:
$10.00

'm sorry if I misled you with that title. Anyone expecting the details of a no-holds-barred hot-oil death-match between James Carville and Al Franken can just skip this chapter. Nor is this the finals of the annual Democratic ugly-off.

No, this was supposed to be a piece on liberal Gepetto James Carville's new book, *We're Right, They're Wrong*. What I realized by the second chapter of Carville's book, however, is that I had already read it under the title *Rush Limbaugh is a Big Fat Idiot*. That's right — except for a few flourishes, they're virtually the same book! Didn't these two hucksters compare galleys over Renaissance Weekend?

The funniest thing about this phenomenon, though, is that *both* books simultaneously made *The New York Times* bestseller list. Now, I'll admit making the *Times* list with liberal manifestoes like these doesn't exactly require the luck of, say, a Pauly Shore. What's funny, though, is the way these two authors have duped millions of liberal lemmings into buying *both* books. "Hey, this is brilliant honey! But somehow it sounds familiar ... Up for a game of Uno?"

There are *some* differences between the two, of course. For instance, Franken's is longer by 88 pages and is hardcover. Oh, and did I mention that Carville didn't write his? That's right — just like Hillary, his is ghostwritten (that's like plagiarism without the detention). But hey — it's selling!

So since these two books are so nearly identical, which one gets the nod as the most unctuous liberal screed of the year? Let's put them *mano a mano* and see who's left standing.

BATTLE OF THE LIBERAL PUNDITS

Smugness
Winner: *Franken.* Sorry Jim, you can't beat upper West Side in this category, no matter how many times Mary tells you bald is beautiful.

Humor
Winner: *Franken.* Based solely on the fact that he's met John Belushi (and that embarrassing *Meet the Press* parody Carville attempts).

Franken going strong ...

<u>Preachiness</u>
Winner: *Carville*. He *was* a teacher before whatever he is
now. And let's face it — at heart, Franken knows he's
way out of his league.

<u>Credentials</u>
Winner: *Carville*. He is somewhat respected, and I think
it's clear that if "Rush Limbaugh" wasn't in the title,
Franken's book would currently be sitting in the discount
bin next to *Susan Anton: A Life*.

Tie ballgame, folks ...

<u>Brown-nosing</u>
Winner: *Franken*. Hard to compete with a guy who's
essentially made it his living. Plus, he's the perfect height
for it.

It's Franken by a (brown) nose! (At least I picked the
right book to parody — maybe now I'll get myself a
ghostwriter to handle Carville's).

17

MY DINNER WITH ANDRE

ou know, reading back over some of the stuff I've written already, it occurs to me that you might get the impression that I hate all liberals. But that, of course, is not the case. Realistically, I try not to *hate* anyone (and just as realistically, I don't succeed in that).

Nonetheless, as far as liberals go, I only find fault with the loudmouths, the phonies, the sanctimonious types who talk too loud in restaurants and ramble on and on about achieving "equity in society" while they own $500 dogs. You know — Franken types.

But as I said, I certainly do not hate all liberals. Take my brother-in-law, for instance.

My brother-in-law is as liberal as they come — just my luck, my sister is attracted to these pullover-sweater types. His name is Andre (how liberal can you get?). Andre works as a lawyer, but not the sue-first-ask-questions-later type. I have to admit, Andre backs his schtick up. He's always doing pro-bono legal work, he works at a food bank, he's even a volunteer fireman (where he's not exactly surrounded by the wine-and-cheese crowd). To be painfully honest, if more liberals were like this guy, I probably couldn't have written this book (what a loss to Western letters *that* would've been, huh?).

Anyway, Andre is a guy I like and respect. We have my sister and him over for dinner occasionally, and while I always scrupulously avoid politics (particularly as he's always pushing this "political action committee" he's part of — whoever heard of "Democrats for Sloths?"), I'm afraid that recently, I lapsed. To be blunt: we got into it over the meatloaf.

I guess it was bound to happen; never invite a liberal to dinner during an election year. I don't know who started it, although I do remember saying something along the lines of "anyone who would vote for that philandering draft-dodger must have the brain of a dung-beetle," causing my wife to administer an under-the-table karate-chop to my thigh that would have split a cinder block. Anyway, harsh words were exchanged, and while nobody actually threw any food, let's just say dessert was a trifle — strained.

One of the things Andre kept bringing up to me was the fact that I'm not as involved, politically, as he is. "And what do you do?" he asked me, after I'd compared his social activism to my dog's habit of chasing his tail. "All you do is sit around reading *The Hockey News* and those how-to-retire-early books."

Now, while I deny this completely, I suddenly found I could no longer resist pulling out my hole card. See, Andre didn't know about this book contract I had. And that's one thing Andre hasn't done. He may read *Mother Jones* and *The New Yorker* cover-to-cover, but he has never written an entire book.

I confess, I dropped my manuscript-in-progress down before him feeling like Moses delivering the Ten Commandments. At least it shut him up for awhile.

Anyway, after reading through the entire thing right there at the table, occasionally throwing me appalled looks while my sister tried to stare me to death, he turned the last page and pronounced that he had never read anything so "negative," and that I was "a man with a lot of unresolved hostility."

Now as I said, I like Andre, but that's the sort of psychobabble that makes my eyes swivel in my head. Frankly, it was all I could do not to bank a crumbcake off his skull (of course, as Andre is also an accomplished martial artist, this would have been a highly imprudent move on my part). Nonetheless, when the smoke cleared and tempers cooled, we parted friends, even laughing over the fact that I had told him he was "doomed to a life of supporting quiche-eating degenerates who didn't give a rat's ass about him." I mean, what's negative about that?

However, because he's an intelligent guy, I admit that some of what Andre said gave me pause. And after looking back over the manuscript, I decided that maybe he was right. Just as I don't want to give the impression that I hate all liberals, the book did seem a tad ... disapproving.

So I thought I might take a moment to make one point: I believe in the American political system. Yes, it has got its faults, and yes, it allows for characters like Richard Gephardt to inflict themselves upon millions regularly. Nonetheless, I think it's the best system ever devised. See, that's why Andre and I were able to part friends. Because we both know that, at heart, at least we share *that* opinion.

And while it doesn't always happen, I think that most of

the time, the people elected feel a responsibility to their constituents. Most of the people who serve in public office, whether conservative *or* liberal, do have their hearts in the right place, and if they don't, I don't believe they manage to last very long. Maybe I'm naive. I hope not. Because I really believe that the vast majority of the people in public office get there because they actually *deserve* to be there, for one reason or another.

And then, of course, there's Marion Barry.

18
MARION BARRY
AND COLON HYDROTHERAPY

was watching CNN the other day (which I'll only do until Rupert Murdoch gets his news channel up and running), when they reported that Marion Barry would be excusing himself from his duties as Mayor of Washington, D.C. in order to go "on retreat" in search of "spiritual renewal." In all honesty, my immediate thoughts were, "Uh oh, he's back on the pipe."

Then one of Barry's traditional apologists, Rock Newman, came on with what I thought would be some sort of explanation; instead, Newman talked around the issue and dropped hints about Barry's troubles, finally stating when pressed that he wouldn't "confirm, deny, verify or otherwise whether relapse has taken place or not." Then I thought, "Alright, Rock — so why the hell are you on my television set?"

Newman, for those of you unfamiliar with this Goliath of political insight, is more commonly known as a professional boxing promoter, a sport whose governance and standards of behavior can best be compared to the average Caracas cockfighting syndicate.* The fact that Newman was the Mayor's campaign advisor and head of his transition team during Barry's miraculously-successful run for re-election is proof enough of the state of things in Washington, D.C. these days. But what bothered me even more than Barry's apparently unlimited license to screw-up on the job (a license few politicians enjoy) was this New Age twaddle His Honor used to get himself off the hook.

"**Spiritual renewal**"? What the hell is this "spiritual renewal"? Is that like renewing a library book? Are you telling me all I have to do is take a few weeks off and go somewhere where they stamp "renewed" on my forehead, and then I can come back to work with all my screw-ups forgotten? Wow. And all these years, I've been worried about getting fired! That's some trick, that spiritual renewal.

I guess what we're supposed to believe here is that this heartfelt soul-searching is an example of the "new" Marion Barry — as opposed to the old, less-eloquent one, the one whose response to the cops who busted him was simply, "that bitch set me up."

Now, we don't know precisely why it is that Barry decided to flee the D.C area — and his job — again; I'm

---

* Newman made headlines again recently at a fight between his boxer Riddick Bowe and Andrew Golota. Immediately following the fight, Newman leapt into the ring and charged Golota, a brilliant move that caused a melee that injured 14 and led to 16 arrests.

Let's do a little comparison here. Rock Newman advised Barry on his campaign, Jeane Kirkpatrick is advising Bob Dole on his campaign. Can you imagine Kirkpatrick hiking up her skirt and leaping into a boxing ring in order to precipitate such an event? Somehow, it doesn't quite seem feasible. Keeping company with a campaign advisor who is comfortable inciting riots on national TV may explain why Marion Barry has never quite been considered a serious Presidential threat.

sure we'll never know. But apparently, because he couched his parting shot in such New Age vernacular as **spiritual rejuvenation**, we're expected to nod our heads in approval, admiring a man who keeps such a watchful eye on his **wholeness and health**. "That Marion, he sure is one highly-evolved individual," we're supposed to be telling each other. Perhaps if he had told the cops, "Wait! I'm suffering **relapse symptoms**, officers," when they burst in on him as he lit that crack pipe, they would have just given him a reassuring little hug and let him go.

Anyway, I sat there staring at my television awhile, wondering what horrible crimes Washingtonians committed in their former lives that they're now saddled with this operator. But after watching the deferential coverage the networks accorded this event, I realized something.

You know what? The point of the ongoing Barry sideshow is not his unfitness for office. It's not even the considerable damage he's done to the public image of black politicians, damage amplified by the symbolic nature of his role as Mayor of our nation's capital. The real disaster here is the liberal-inspired atmosphere of indulgence which allows such catch-all bullshit as "spiritual renewal" to serve as acceptable public discourse. This attitude of perfect permissiveness, of no standards whatsoever, has led to an America where one of our most prominent mayors knows he can hide behind the sound-byte equivalent of "abracadabra." I tell you, it made me cranky.

You think I'm being too harsh on his Honor? Are things that bad in D.C.? Well, consider:

- The emergency 911 system doesn't work;

- Two-thirds of the city's police cars are out of service;

- D.C. has the highest crime rate of any city or state in America;

- Washington, D.C. spends more per pupil than any state in the Union, yet its students rank dead last in reading and math. There isn't even money for substitute teachers;

- Due to poorly-operating treatment plants, the water is undrinkable, and the city has issued numerous warnings to boil it before use;

- Only 40 of the city's 104 garbage trucks work;

- Recently, 1,500 traffic signals were not functioning because the city had failed to pay its electric bill;

- Street conditions have been so bad, buses often make up their routes as they go, depending on what streets they can manage to drive on;

- D.C. has $3 billion in long-term debt.

Is that incredible? Calcutta sounds cozier. Meanwhile, we're supposed to get all warm and gooey because Marion's taken off for Lourdes. Puh-lease.

Now, I know it's been said before, but I've just got to ask: How did they vote this guy in again? Was that ever explained? Wasn't the fact that, as his city deteriorated around him, he was busy smoking crack in a hotel room with an ex-girlfriend (Barry is married), wasn't that just a teeny-tiny tip that his priorities weren't in order? Did they think the fact that he wore a dashiki during the campaign meant he was now capable of solving the budget problem?

This question so puzzled me — after all, somebody in Washington, D.C. must have a memory — that I decided to look into this Barry thing a little deeper. And Jesus, is this guy a piece of work.

First of all, this is not the Mayor's first "spiritual renewal." Barry has had his soul stamped "renewed" so often it's starting to look like Henry Kissinger's passport. How about this quote, from a 1988 *Washington Post*:

> D.C. Mayor Marion Barry, expressing deep concern about his health, said yesterday he spent his week in seclusion countering job-related stress with aerobics, health treatments, Zen meditation and long walks.

Sound familiar? Then try this, from a 1990 *Post*:

> Marion Barry, return(ed) with a flourish to the city ... yesterday. "I'm back ... I feel good about myself ... The difference you will notice in me will be that my life will be more balanced now ... I realize I must spend more time on myself, my family, and engaging in positive, constructive leisure activities."

And now, in 1996:

> "I've come back more physically and more mentally rejuvenated but, more importantly, more spiritually connected with God," he said. "I come back more rested, with more energy, with clearer vision, and more determined than ever before to transform our D.C. government."

Uh, Marion, is this one of your Zen mantras, or are you actually trying to tell us something?

But Barry is apparently willing to do more than just talk the talk. The list of "therapies" this guy has tried makes Woody Allen look like Arnold Schwarzenegger. He has meditated, reconnected, soul-searched, navel-gazed, you name it.

The site of Barry's latest junket out of town, for instance, features a "prayer labyrinth," a 75-foot-wide series of landscaped paths in which the meandering devotee is expected to "shed" the corporal concerns of life while achieving "illumination" and "union with a higher power" (it's a *hedge*, for God's sake!). And when Barry disappeared

during his third mayoral term — this time without explanation — he was later unearthed in a place called Neversink, NY, where he jogged, meditated, and underwent something called *colon hydrotherapy* (now there's a mental image). He also had himself entirely coated in paraffin wax in order to draw out his body's "impurities." Gee, Marion — maybe you should just buy yourself a nice puppy.

So how did he get back in office, you're still wondering? Easy. Barry mobilized the forgotten constituency: criminals.

During his campaign, Barry and his supporters went to the various prisons in the D.C. area and, among other things, promised the inmates repealed or lightened sentences, early parole, jobs in an agency he would form called "Office of Offender Affairs" (to be staffed entirely by convicts), and something called "gate money," which essentially amounted to giving the cons a little walking-around cash upon their release (I swear, I am not making this up). All the crooks had to do, since they couldn't vote themselves, was to make sure their relatives voted for Marion. He also promised out more government jobs than anybody since Huey Long (currently, one of every nine D.C. residents works for the city).

So why aren't condemnations of this character pouring in from all sides? Why aren't the press and Barry's fellow politicos collectively force-feeding him a reality quarter-pounder? Because thanks to where liberalism has finally taken public dialogue in America, *Barry knows* he can get away with almost anything as long as he throws around terms like **reconnect** and **higher power**. Say what you want about Marion, but he's learned how the game is played. Why else would he get off the plane in St. Louis on his way to his **retreat**, ostentatiously reading a Bible? Marion knows a photo op when he sees one. I'm only surprised he wasn't singing "Kumbaya."

All this because a media atmosphere that respects, even exalts this vacuous Shirley MacLaine-ism has let Barry do it to Washington again. I imagine that by now every time rational Washingtonians hear Barry talking **meditation**, they feel like Ned Beatty catching a hint of banjo music on the wind.

You know, in a way, I almost admire his chutzpah. Who knew this dodge would actually work? Nixon should have forgotten that "I-am-not-a-crook" crap; he should have just

> It is one thing to be pristine pure, but how can you really encourage young men and women who are down in the gutter if you have no skeletons in your closet?
> — Bill Clinton's favorite poet Maya Angelou, on what makes Marion Barry more qualified than candidates who haven't served time.

told *The Washington Post* he had **mental fatigue** and needed **renewed faith**. Let Woodward or Bernstein run *that* quote.

"I've been to Moscow and China, but I've never been to me," President Nixon said today, his eyes misting over. For the record, this reporter knows exactly where he's coming from.

Come to think of it, this strategy is a defense lawyer's dream. "My client was suffering **physical and spiritual relapse**," Johnnie Cochran should have told the jury, saving us all a lot of aggravation. "I've got **character defects**, and need to **reconnect myself spiritually with the God of my understanding**," Jim Tucker should have told his Whitewater jury. Maybe the Unabomber can use the **renew** and **strengthen** defense. "Your honor, I took a **fearless moral inventory**, and I find I need **spiritual reconnection**. Waddaya say?" Hey, it could work — he just has to get the trial moved to Washington, D.C.

So **twelve steps** later, we're still stuck with Marion Barry as the Mayor of our nation's capital, a man who seriously expects his constituents to care about the state of his personal karma while their city goes straight into the toilet (thank *God* I don't own an apartment in Washington, D.C.). You know what? The saddest thing here is that Barry's constituents are only getting what they deserve. The next time they can't drink the water or the bus doesn't show up, they should forget about complaining; they'll just have to re-align their **personhood** and head off for some **mental and physical rejuvenation**.

As for myself, I can't wait to try this gimmick. The next time my tax return is due, I'm going to disappear for some "spiritual renewal." If I don't feel like working, I'm heading off somewhere for a few weeks of "spiritual renewal" (preferably somewhere sunny). The bank wants this month's mortgage payment? Spiritual renewal, baby. Hey, if they don't like it, maybe I can get Rock Newman to explain it to them.

(The **bolded terms** were all used at least once by Barry during the press conference he gave upon his return from his most recent retreat. The Mayor received a standing ovation).

19

"ROGER, WE HARDLY KNEW YE"

f there is one area in which Bill Clinton has let America down, it is in his obligation, as a Democrat occupying the White House, to provide America with the official First Buffoon. I'm speaking, of course, of that time-honored tradition, begun during the Carter Administration, of a Democratic President's brother being a bubba dimwit who behaves publicly in ways that would make Gomer Pyle wince. Because while Roger Clinton teased us all with an auspicious beginning (who can forget his early greatness? His Secret Service nickname, "Headache"; his public fistfights; his Deputy Dawg imitation; his disastrous rock band, "Politics"; his shotgun wedding), he has since slipped quietly from the spotlight. Roger, you are no Billy Carter.

Now clearly the Democrats haven't had a monopoly on embarrassing Presidential relatives during recent years. Neil Bush was right in the middle of one of the biggest disasters of the S&L scandal. And the Reagan brood has at times seemed like a bad seed competition; thankfully, Ron Jr. has given up on his ballet ambitions, even if sister Patty is still looking to kickbox nude on the Playboy Channel. But when it comes to the relative who truly distinguished himself in the media age as Chief Executive Jackass, it was the (alas) late Billy Carter who set the standard. Hell, Billy created the role. Who can forget his taking a leak outside at the airport? His racist and anti-Semitic cracks? How about "Billy Beer," unopened six-packs of which now sell as collectors items? Remember his cutting deals with Libya? While his brother was trying to stabilize the Middle East? Amazing.

And disheartening. At least Chelsea's doing her job; she's got the Amy Carter thing down pat. But Roger is slacking, big-time. In fact, if he doesn't start acting-up soon, he could lose First Buffoon status altogether, and the Democrats would have to import Bryant Gumbel to fill the vacancy (one jackass is as good as the next). So concerned am I about this possibility, I've put together a few suggestions for Roger, to help him work his way back into top-boob form.

1. Do an exercise video. We all know obesity is a continuing problem in America, and who better to preach about discovering fitness than a guy raised on Cheez Whiz and fried Spam sandwiches?

2. Become a Not Ready for Prime Time Player. Since 1980, if there is one sure-fire way of making an annoying ass of yourself, this is it. At least if he goes this route, nobody will laugh at him.

3. Get a talk show. The list of unlikely characters who have conned their way into their own talk shows is a who's who of American irrelevancy: Chevy Chase, Danny Bonaduce, Tempest Bledsoe, that fat chick from Wilson Phillips. Roger needs to get his own show and take on the tough issues, dammit!

4. Do an infomercial for the Roger Clinton Abdominal Crunchmeister. Every First Buffoon needs a product to attach his name to. After all, the original had Billy Beer. Roger needs to hire Suzanne Somers and Cher to *ooh* and *aah* as he does sit-ups with some sort of plastic contraption strapped to his belly.

5. Write a book. Oops, he tried that one. *Growing Up Clinton*, unfortunately, wasn't the blockbuster Summit Group Publishing thought it would be. During Roger's book tour (for which he reportedly demanded limo service and a stipend of $6,000 a month), bookstore employees actually had to impersonate customers lining up to get their books signed by "the literary Clinton." Otherwise, all the TV cameras would have shown was an empty bookshop, a few bored workers, and some guy who looked like the President sitting alone at a table, picking his nose with a pen.

6. Become a professional boxer. For some reason, every moe out there who gets bored with his career eventually ends up trying this one. If it's good enough for Mickey Rourke and Mark Gastineau, it's certainly good enough for Roger. And if this doesn't work, there's always pro wrestling (an Arkansas favorite).

7. Start a psychic hot line. Celebrity relatives have staked this area out as their turf, and Roger is entitled to his taste of the action. In the grand tradition of LaToya Jackson and Jacqueline Stallone, Roger could set himself up as a phone-in counselor and tell his fans how they can live successful, exciting lives. After all, it's worked for Roger, hasn't it?

So get on the stick, Roger — your country needs you. You can't expect Bill to cover all this territory alone!

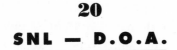

20

Every generation has its peculiar curses. My grandparents had World War II and rationing. My parents had Vietnam and Joan Baez. Watching an old *Saturday Night Live* on Comedy Central the other day, I figured out what my generation's curse is.

You see, I grew up on the old *Saturday Night Live* episodes. I remember my first one vividly, lying on the couch half-asleep on what seemed very late on a Saturday night, when suddenly these two guys in black suits were on the screen, one chubby, one slim. They started dancing wildly to this fast r&b number, then the chubby one started singing in a raspy, strangled voice. It was just so strange, so unlike what one was used to seeing on television, that I was instantly awake. What was going on? Was this serious or a joke? Did somebody take over the television studio at gunpoint? Who in the world were these guys?

From that moment on, I was hooked, as were so many others across the country. I followed the show religiously, watched it all the way through to the end every time, even the one Bea Arthur hosted. I mean, I was such a fan, I knew who Al Franken was in *1978*. Incredible, right? My friends and I — hell, my generation — we looked to SNL to tell us what was hip, what was ridiculous, what was worthwhile and what was bullshit. It was, to a teenager, like having a bunch of wild friends your parents didn't know about, and probably wouldn't have approved of.

So you can imagine what it's been like for me, and many like me, to watch what's happened to most of the *Saturday Night* cast members, and to the show itself. Let's face it, Keith Richards has aged better. I stopped watching SNL a long time ago, after they started letting guys like Alex Karras host, but before the show itself had become a punch line. I'd vaguely heard that Al Franken had progressed from just writing to being a featured SNL player, and when I finally happened to catch a few minutes of a recent show, I remembered why I'd stopped watching in the first place. The whole production was like seeing your grandfather trying to demonstrate his World War II judo moves.

Of course, this hasn't been all Al's fault. Let's give credit where it's due. Once, during the TV writers' strike in 1981, Al and his buddy Tom Davis even volunteered to write a whole episode of SNL on their own. I mean, that showed dedication, it really did — they were trying to save the show, it was admirable. The fact that Producer Dick Ebersol took one look at the script and canceled the rest of *Saturday Night Live's* season, well, that's not really the point. That's nitpicking, is what that is. At least Ebersol promised the boys they could host the following season's opening show. And why he then didn't return their phone calls in the months that followed, I don't think that's relevant either. That's just show biz, I guess. I really wouldn't know.

And there have been some bright moments, there really have — Eddie Murphy, Dennis Miller, I even laughed at Brad Hall once. As I remember, he fell down or something. But other than that, things have gotten pretty lean over at 30 Rock. Maybe if they cut Lorne Michaels' salary a bit, they could at least get Garrett back. And I doubt Laraine Newman's very busy. Hey, I bet Tim Kazurinsky is free. These are just ideas I'm throwing out. But let's face it, they couldn't hurt.

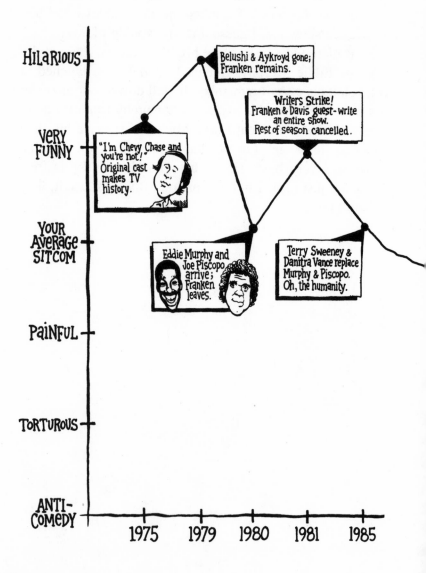

21

THE BIMBO PATROL RIDES AGAIN!

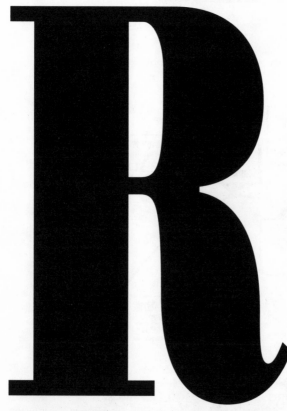

emember the Bimbo Patrol? That was one of the less-publicized aspects of the 1992 Clinton campaign. Well guess what? It's baaaaaack ...

In 1992, the Clinton campaign, headed by chief strategist James Carville, recognized that it had what it termed a "bimbo problem." This information, incredibly, came from the Clinton campaign itself; one morning, a Clinton campaign staffer startled everyone at a press conference by blithely announcing that she had been assigned to something called a "bimbo patrol," designed to counteract expected "bimbo eruptions" (i.e., women claiming to have slept with the then-Governor of Arkansas).

Now, coming on the heels of the taped conversations between Clinton and Gennifer Flowers, you would think that the implications of all this would be clear, and that America's voters would have gotten the hint; any guy needing his own "bimbo patrol" is pure sleaze. The problem, however, was not so much that the voters didn't get the hint, it's that they didn't get the information.

You see, except for the occasional unexpected mention during interviews, the press turned quite a blind eye to this whole thing. It really wasn't much of a story outside of Washington, D.C. Here was the married Governor of Arkansas, already taped on the phone with one woman, setting up a special task force to counteract future charges he knew he'd be facing. Can you imagine the conversation that must have led to this?

Carville: Well, sir, how many extra-marital affairs have you actually had?

Clinton: In this area code?

According to Mary Matalin, Deputy Chairman of George Bush's 1992 campaign (and James Carville's *wife*), at least $28,000 was spent by the Democrats on this "bimbo patrol."

Private investigators were used, sources were investigated and attacked, reporters were swayed; God knows what else went on. The source of the money was never disclosed, so where it actually all went is also anybody's guess.

From there, all necessary denials and counter-attacks on the "bimbo" issue were fed to a pliant press corp by Clinton campaign mouthpiece George Stephanopoulos. And in the middle of it all was James Carville, leftist Svengali, spinning reams of "disinformation" on his way to saddling us with one of his fellow pork salesmen for a President. You've got to admit, he did a helluva job — it couldn't have been easy.

This time around, however, Carville's role has taken on a somewhat more shadowy tone. Here we are, in mid-1996, and the Clinton people have yet to announce an official job for James, the man who made Clinton king. While Carville himself has avowed unequivocally that he "is part of this campaign," he is no longer chief campaign advisor; that gig went to political gun-for-hire Dick Morris. And so, like George Stephanopoulos before him, James has been kicked somewhere downstairs by the regime he helped install.

Well, given what went on last time, I think it's pretty clear what James and his lil' buddy George are going to be doing this election. It's just that nobody wants to *say* it.

I guess Bill must sleep well in his bed these nights, knowing "the boys" are out there keeping his image clean. That is, if he ever does actually *sleep* in bed.

Bimbo Patrol First Officer Jimmy "Carv" Carville sat in the squad car, staring out into the Washington, D.C. night. It looked like it was going to be a long one. He took a sip of coffee. "Quiet night, so far," he said in his trademark Cajun twang.

His partner, Bimbo Patrolman George "Steph" Stephanopoulos, was at the wheel. Steph nodded absently. "I was just thinking about last time," he said, his voice dreamy. He was much younger than Carville, barely looking old enough to drive; as it was, his head scarcely cleared the steering wheel, despite the phone books he was sitting on.

"You're thinkin' about last time? What, the '92 election?" Carville asked him.

"Yeah," Steph replied. "We had some time, didn't we? Chasin' off all those press guys. How about that time with Brit Hume, remember that?"

"Damned if I don't!" Carville said, a huge grin splitting his slightly inbred face. "Was that a close one or wasn't it? We beat that ol' Brit Hume by about one minute!" Carville gave a little chuckle. "And let me tell you, that little filly, she woulda made a heap of trouble, woulda spilled her guts. Was sure a good thing we got there first."

"Yeah," Steph said. "That Brit Hume, he's trouble."

"I know it. A real pain in my butt. He ain't with us, know what I mean? He don't do the right thing." Jimmy Carville shook his head in disgust, then took another pull on his coffee. It was the conservative reporters, the Brit Humes of the world, that made his job that much tougher.

Suddenly the car's radio sprang to life. "*BP One, BP One, come in BP One ...*" Steph reached for the radio as Carville let out a little whoop. "Hot damn, youngblood — here we go!"

Their first call was in a trailer park, just north of the D.C. limits. Once they found the right trailer, Carv knocked lightly on the rusty door and opened it without even waiting for a reply.

The smell of stale beer and cheap perfume hit them full in the face. Inside, the place was a mess, a clutter of *Glamour* magazines, dirty dishes, and women's clothing. There was a giant "Bill Clinton in '96" poster covering one whole wall. Sitting on a daybed before it, sobs shaking her body, was a woman in a frayed pink bathrobe.

She hadn't even looked up when they'd entered. "'Scuse me, ma'am," Carv said. When she didn't respond, Carv put a bit more into it. "'*Scuse me*, ma'am."

This time she looked up. Steph saw that underneath the streaked mascara, she was pretty, in a big-eyed-and-hopeful sort of way. Blond, of course. He figured her for a waitress. Why did they always have to be so young? "Are — are you the newspaper guys?" she asked in a quavering voice.

"No, ma'am, that we're not," Carv said levelly. "No ma'am. See, we're sort of with *him*," he said, fingering his BP badge, which showed a picture of a smiling Bill Clinton with the words "Four More Years!" embossed beneath it. "Now, why don't we talk about this thing a bit? You don't want to fly off the handle and do something rash now, do you?" Carv's voice was the epitome of reason and understanding.

Before the girl could answer, however, there was the sound of another car arriving on the gravel outside. "We got company, Carv," Steph said.

"Ah, hell," Carville groaned. "Steph, why don't you make sure the young lady's alright. I'll be right back." With that, Carv stepped out the door.

Steph didn't have to go outside to know what would

happen next; he'd seen Carv work before. First Carville
would greet the reporter like an old friend, even if he'd
never seen him before. "You're new around here, ain't you?
What paper you from? Oh yeah? Ain't that Bob Cantwell's
beat? Whatever happened to ol' Bob? Moved to New York,
huh? The upper West Side? You don't say!" Then, after the
small talk, Carv would slide in the pitch, real gentle. "Look,

I know your boss, the chief editor. He's a good friend of mine. *Good* friend. Comes to all our fund-raisers." The guy wouldn't miss the implied threat of *that*. "You look like a nice guy. You a Dem? 'Course you are! Look, this here, this thing with this lil' girl, this is nothing ..."

Steph could never get over how Carville could do it, how he could sweet-talk his way into the granite hearts of these press guys. "This girl, she's just a tramp looking for a little publicity, a little excitement in her life," Carv would tell the guy. "There's nothing here, no proof, nothing. I'd tell you if there was, I swear I would." Then the arm around the shoulder. "Tell you what," he'd say now, with that big Cajun grin of his. "You come around the White House around election time, around when things are really happening, and I'll see you get some good stuff. Some inside, *exclusive* stuff. Ya'll read me?" Then he'd take the guy's card, give him a little wink to send him off, and the reporter would leave feeling like he'd just cultivated the next Deep Throat, visions of Pulitzers in his head. Ten seconds later Carv would throw the card over his shoulder and forget he'd ever laid eyes on the man.

Suddenly alone with the sobbing woman in the trailer, Steph went the paternal route. "Someone looks like they could use some coffee," he said brightly, looking around for something that might resemble a coffee pot. "You got any around here?"

The girl nodded in an almost childlike way and pointed towards the peeling cupboard. "Okay, that's great," Steph said, in that boyish, earnest way he had. "Now why don't you tell me —" He was interrupted by Carville coming back inside.

"Alright, that's *that*," Carville said, tearing up a business card and dropping it into the general mess of the place.

"Now let's get to the point, enough jackin' around. You listening, missy?" Carv's voice was not loud, but there was no mistaking the firmness there now. He didn't sound like a man ready to negotiate.

The girl nodded, her eyes gone wide. "Okay, here's what it is. You're gonna forget you ever knew that man" — he pointed to the big Clinton poster — "ever met him, ever saw him a day in your life, you understand me?" The girl didn't respond, but Carv clearly had her attention. Her bottom lip was trembling slightly. "Yeah, I know, I know," Carville said dismissively, waving a hand. "He told you he loved you, told you he could do things for you, told you he would never forget you. Well, guess what? He did forget you. And now you're gonna forget him, you understand?" The girl seemed to sit up a bit, her back stiffening. Steph was surprised. Was she going to put up a fight?

"You're gonna forget him!" Carv said harshly, and the girl shrank back. "'Cause one thing he told you is true, and that's that he is a very powerful man. He — *we* — can make more trouble for you than you ever thought existed, you hear?" The girl sunk into the daybed now, looking as if she'd shrunk to half her size. "You got no choice. You just forget the whole thing!"

The girl was starting to tear up a bit, and Carville softened. "Look," he said, more gently. "Why you want to hurt the Chief? Why'd you want to go and call that 'ol newspaper for? The Chief, he's a good man, he done right by you, I'm sure. You had fun with him, right? He treated you like a lady?" She began to nod slightly as he spoke. "It's just that sometimes, a man in his position, being President and all, he makes promises he can't really deliver on."

"He told me he was gonna get a divorce for me!" she suddenly cried. "That I was gonna be the First Lady! And he ain't even *called* me since!" She started sobbing again, even louder than before. "All he left me with is his big ol' boxer drawers and a half a bucket of chicken!"

"Oh, Jesus," Carv said, rolling his eyes at Steph. This one was going to take a while.

It had gone like that all night, until well after midnight, the boys playing good-cop/bad-cop or using whatever means they had to put out the fires. There had been nurses, hotel chambermaids, congressional interns, Georgetown coeds. It seemed like every source they had, every mole in every press room, was checking in with a tip tonight. "Wow," Steph had said at one point, slightly awed as yet another call came in. "Seems like the Chief's been pretty busy."

"No wonder his Missus is lookin' to adopt," Carv said with a wink. "She could probably use the company."

Now it was almost two in the morning, and the boys sat in the B.P. squad car, sipping the eternal coffees. They were dog-tired, but in a job-well-done kind of way. They'd just finished a tough one — a stewardess who lived deep in the heart of *Washington Times* territory. "Those Moonies'll bury us!" Steph had blurted when it came over the radio. At the last minute, Carv had managed to get the reporter to take a rain check by giving him the address of the "entertainment establishment" where Dick Morris spends his lunch hours.

Now, mercifully, the radio had gone quiet, and the boys were enjoying the relative peace. "Carv, let me ask you something," Steph finally said, his head resting back against the seat. "How come you were so hard on that little girl tonight, that first one?"

"You mean that trailer trash?" Carv said, also resting back, his eyes half-closed.

"Yeah."

"Well, I'll tell you," Carv began, his voice thoughtful. "See, I been at this long enough, seen enough of 'em by now to know the types. That lil' girl, she was scared as a rabbit, didn't know what she was doin'. And see, she really loved the Chief — she didn't even want any of the kitty money. The Chief, he has that effect on people. She was just *lookin'* for an excuse to call the whole thing off. So I gave her one."

Steph didn't say anything; he seemed preoccupied as he played with his decoder ring. "Carv, can I ask you something?" he said after awhile. "You're no spring chicken, you've been around a bit and then some. Doesn't it get you down? I mean, all we do is stop one bimbo, just so another one can come crawling out of the woodwork. I mean, where does it end?"

Carv seemed to think this one over a bit. "You know why I do it son?" he said finally. "I know this may sound corny, but I don't care. It ain't for the Democrats. It ain't even for the country. It's for William Jefferson Clinton. This man, you don't meet too many like him. Take it from me, George ..." Carv only called his partner "George" when the elder man was deadly serious. "I been around politics a long time, a lot longer than you. I seen 'em come, and I seen 'em go. But Bill Clinton, he's the real thing, the rarest thing. A man of integrity. I never met a man that inspires me like the Chief does."

Steph was staring at his partner, riveted; he hadn't seen Carv this emotional since they cancelled Hee-Haw. Carville gave a little shrug. "I know he don't seem that way to some. But once you're in with him, you're part of the family. I thought I was beyond caring by now ..." here he gave an embarrassed wave. "But I would do anything for this man. And he would do anything for me. That's why I wear this badge, son. And that's why you wear yours. It's a *trust* thing, is what it is," he said solemnly. "Mutual trust."

Steph nodded, thinking back wistfully to the first time he'd laid eyes on the Chief himself. It was about five years ago. He'd been standing on a corner in downtown Little Rock when the Chief came along and asked him if he needed someone to hold his hand while he crossed the street. By the time they reached the other side, Steph had signed on with the Chief's campaign.

"That's why I'll never forgive myself for letting him down like that," Carv went on. "He trusted me. I'll never forgive myself for blowing that Gennifer Flowers thing. I mean, I almost cost the man the election."

"Aw, Carv, come on man, don't be so hard on yourself. You got to let that one go. Nobody could have stopped — "

"I almost blew the damn election!" Carville said forcefully. Then he gave a weary sigh. "Ah, I don't know, maybe I'm just gettin' old," he said. "I shoulda seen that one comin'. Paula Jones, well hell, that was off my watch, the Chief was elected already when that one broke. But that bitch Flowers, I just — " Carv's voice tightened. Steph didn't know what to say. The elder man looked off into the distance, his face betraying his emotions as he replayed the 1992 election in his misshapen head for the thousandth time.

Then his face split into his usual grin. "That 'ol Chief, he just can't keep his wick dry! Well, good 'ol boys is good 'ol boys, I always say. Thank God it all worked out. C'mon, pretty boy," he said, revving the car's engine. "Let's head over to the all-nighter and get us some ribs."

"Do they have chicken, you think?" Steph asked as they pulled out onto the deserted street. "I'm off red meat."

The older man just shook his head. "Youngblood," he said, with his wicked grin. "You got a lot to learn."

Steph was picking at his light salad, no dressing, when the "Code Three" came through. As soon as he heard those two words over the portable radio, Carv stuffed a few barbecued ribs into his back pocket and bolted through the diner's front door. Steph wasn't far behind him.

"C'mon, Steph — double time!" Carv shouted from the front seat of the squad, as Steph hopped in and started her up. Steph gave her the gun and the car lurched away from the curb with a screech.

Neither of them said a word as they raced down K Street, but both men knew what the other was thinking. *A Code Three*. They'd never fielded one of these before — not even last election. A Code Three meant an emergency, something unusual. There could be a reporter on the scene already. Or it could be ...

"Brit Hume," Steph said as they raced down the street, the concern in his voice audible. "Carv, this feels like Brit Hume."

"Now don't go jumpin' no guns, blood. We don't know that yet. This could be anything." He gave Steph a quick sidelong glance, to make sure the younger man was in control. He looked okay, his jaw set, his eyes intent on the road ahead of them, his feet dangling over the edge of the seat where they just barely reached the pedals. *He's coming along fine*, Carv thought. *He's a good driver too, although he can't park for shit.* "We don't know that it's him," the older man said. "But it don't feel good, I'll give you that."

They pulled into the parking lot of the *Motel Splendor* with the squad car's lights out, creeping along slowly. "Okay, easy does it now, easy ..." Carv said as he eyed the dark and apparently lifeless old motel. Then Carv's experienced eyes seemed to catch something. "Kill the engine!" he hissed.

Carv got out of the car, moving quietly and in slow motion, and Steph followed his lead. Carv took a few steps towards the motel, towards the row of rooms stretching away from them in the dark. Then he pointed. That's when Steph saw it; one of the doors was slightly open.

They crept towards it. Steph didn't dare breathe. He found himself wishing he was somewhere else, somewhere safe and familiar — back home in bed or in the White House Press Room, feeding Blitzer his lines for the day. He looked around them now for anything unusual, any clues as to what they were getting themselves into. There was nothing there, except for a few parked cars in the deserted lot. And that open door.

Carv crept forward, moving as surely and silently in the dark as a cat. He waved for Steph to stand back. Then Carv stepped to the door.

Crouched low, looking like every muscle in his body was poised to spring, Carv gave the door a solid nudge. It swung open, and Carv went in.

The first thing Steph was aware of was the sound of Carv's voice in his ears. "Chief on the scene! Chief on the scene!" Carv was yelling, before Steph could see what was happening. Steph didn't hesitate. His training took over immediately, and as Carv slammed the door shut Steph turned and positioned himself before it, blocking the way in with his body. Steph crossed his arms over his chest. With the Chief himself on the scene, any reporters showing up now would have to go through all five-feet-plus of George Stephanopoulos.

Carville was inside the room now, and Steph couldn't tell what was happening. Was Carv alright? Was the Chief alright? What was going on? With the Chief himself there, that explained the Code Three — anytime the Chief was directly involved was a Code Three. But was there anything else? Steph could barely make out the murmur of voices inside the room. All he'd had time to glimpse before Carv slammed the door shut was a battered dresser with the Chief's telltale bucket of Kentucky Fried Chicken on it.

It was torture, the waiting, the not knowing. Steph's training held, but before long he was debating whether he should leave his post and take a quick look inside.

Then Carv came out, brushing hard past him. "Carv, what —" was all Steph could manage, as Carville headed for the squad car, walking fast. Steph watched him, confused; then he made a quick decision. He had to see what was in that room.

He opened the door slowly, craning his head around it for a quick look.

Steph walked out to the squad car, where Carv sat motionless in the front seat. Steph's head was swimming.

He leaned on the car's roof. "Wow, Carv, I never realized," he said, his sweet, boyish voice filled with wonder. "I mean, I've never seen the Chief at a scene before. And wearing only a pair of boxer drawers too. You know, he's kind of ... *fat*," the younger man said tentatively. "Jeepers, Carv, he's enormous!"

Carville didn't say anything, staring straight ahead in the car's front seat. "Boy, the Chief sure does like his fried chicken," Steph said with a chuckle. "He kinda spit some on me when he started singing along to that radio." Steph ran his fingers through his hair, picking out various chicken parts. "He sure does like that Elvis stuff too. Dancing around and singin' like that."

Carville was still rock motionless in the squad car, but

now his head was down on the dashboard.

Steph's brows knit as something seemed to occur to him. "Hey Carv, how come your wife was in there dancing with the Chief?" he asked. Carville didn't respond. "Carv? How come your wife was dancing with the Chief like that? Is your wife workin' the Patrol now too, Carv? Carv?"

"Oh, God ..." Carville moaned inside the car.

"Carv? How come your wife was dancing with the Chief in there, Carv? Carv? How come your wife was in there dancing with her — "

"WOULD YOU SHUT UP YOU LITTLE ASSHOLE!" Carville screamed, the veins standing out blue on his odd skull. "Just *shut up*. You utter one more sound and I will personally — "

Then the car radio sprang to life.

"BP One, BP One, come in BP One. Okay, I got it. That's 555-1416," came the voice over the radio. Carv hurriedly jotted the number down on a napkin.

Steph stepped back to let Carville out of the car. "Carv? What's the matter? What's going on? Carv? What's that number? Carv?"

"Just shut up and gimme a quarter, will you, Stephanopoulos?" Carville said flatly. Steph handed him one, wide-eyed. "'Cause what I got here," Carville said, waving the napkin, "is Brit Hume's home phone number."

Steph's mouth dropped open in shock, and Carville gave a bitter little laugh. "And take that badge off, will you?" he said, heading for the phone booth across the street. "You look like a real horse's ass."

22

FUN WITH NEXIS

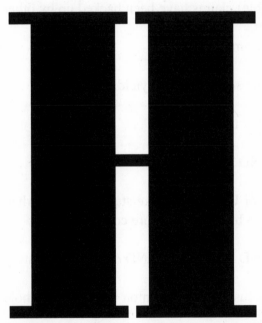

ave you ever heard of Nexis? It's a computer database that houses nearly every major newspaper and magazine worldwide. Nexis allows the user to search the back issues of all these publications by using key words or phrases. You type in the search terms and Nexis retrieves the relevant articles in a few seconds. It's the kind of thing that researchers and editors use when they're not busy taping *Doonesbury* to their refrigerators.

The fun thing about Nexis is testing how many times

certain words or phrases have occurred within the planet's numerous publications. For instance, if you type something as simple as, say, "Al Gore," Nexis will retrieve thousands upon thousands of articles for you (assuredly the dullest collection of writings since Panetta started his diary).

Franken plays with Nexis a bit in his book, so I thought I'd do the same. I figured I'd check up on my own research in the process, and see how many times some of my (perfectly reasonable) claims have been backed up by other enlightened writers.

Let's start with something basic:

Bill Clinton AND *sausage gravy* yields: 4 stories

Not too bad. Let's try

Ted Kennedy AND *boxer shorts*: 23 stories

Okay, the Senator Underpants joke stays. Tell you what, let's play with this a bit and try a more complex search:

Mansa Musa AND *Bill Clinton* AND *conspiracy*: 1 story

Just as I always suspected — Clinton is in on this whole Mansa Musa thing!

Alright, switching gears:

Al Gore AND *Tipper* AND *penis*: 17 stories!

Now, I assume most of those have to do with the *Our Stolen Future* book. If not, God only knows who Tipper and Al have been giving interviews to.

Barney Frank AND *elocution lessons*: 1 story
Barney Frank AND *buffet*: 29 stories

Proving I'm not the only one who's noticed Frank's heat-seeking guidance system for locating an imminent lunch spread.

Alright, as long as we're just sort of hacking along with this, let's take a break from our regularly-scheduled book and jerk around with Nexis awhile (after all, my publisher's picking up the tab) (can't wait to tell him).

Marion Barry AND
>   straightjacket: 18 stories
>   space cadet: 2 stories
>   re-election AND incredible: 42 stories
>   Brooklyn Bridge AND constituents: 1 story
>   Rock Newman AND corrupt: 13 stories
>   that bitch set me up: 104 stories

Roger Clinton AND
>   Jim Varney: 3 stories
>   shotgun wedding: 3 stories
>   Billy Carter AND buffoon: 11 stories

Jesse Jackson AND
>   Nipsey Russell: 7 stories
>   get a job: 466 stories!

Bill Clinton AND
>   chubby: 274 stories
>   wide load: 8 stories
>   McDonalds: 4,851 stories!
(one for each of Bill's visits, I assume)

Bill Clinton AND

        Colonel Sanders: 38 stories
        Paul Prudhomme: 27 stories
        Gomer Pyle: 57 stories
        The Dukes of Hazard: 9 stories
        James Carville AND Deliverance: 23 stories

Democrats AND

        pork: 17,156 stories (gee, what a surprise)
        big government: 13,003 stories (another
        shocker)
        tax-happy: 181 stories
        sloths: 318 stories (?!)
        (What hath Andre wrought?)

Sam Donaldson AND
       toupee: 68 stories
       eyebrows AND frightening: 5 stories
       Star Trek: 103 stories

Warren Christopher AND:
       Star Trek: 46 stories

Stephanopoulos AND:
       boyish: 107 stories
       puberty: 9 stories
       sidekick: 55 stories
       driver's ed: 2 stories
       training wheels: 1 story

Upper West Side AND:
>   Marxism: 31 stories

Leon Panetta AND:
>   riveting: 15 stories
>   Al Gore AND dull: 12 stories
>   personal charisma: 0 stories

What fun! Now let's see how often a few of my heroes have managed to get into articles with the Big Cheese himself:

Bill Clinton AND:
>   Mason Reese: 4 stories
>   Gordie Howe: 34 stories
>   Sonny Chiba: 2 stories
>   Professor Irwin Corey: 6 stories
>   Marty Feldman: 2 stories
>   Ann B. Davis: 9 stories
>   Leon Redbone: 8 stories
>   Bruno Sammartino: 2 stories
>   Menudo: 10 stories
>   Jack Carter: 16 stories
>   Richard Roundtree OR Shaft: 10 stories
>   Shirley Booth OR Hazel: 14 stories
>   Ruth Buzzi: 10 stories
>   Charo: 17
>   Demosthenes Savalas: 0 stories

Those are really the numbers — can you imagine what some of those articles must be about? (Alright, I think you'll agree we better get back to the book now, before I do something that might be considered silly).

23

ADVENTURES IN POLITICS
JUNE 24—28, 1996

MY SEARCH FOR JESSE JACKSON'S JOB, OR HOW I BLOW MY FIRST BIG INTERVIEW BECAUSE LIBERALS DON'T RETURN PHONE CALLS

see that Jesse Jackson now hosts a talk show on CNN — *Both Sides with Jesse Jackson* (as if that's what we're actually going to get). I was glad to see Jesse finally got himself a steady gig, because before this show, I couldn't figure out what he actually did for a living. This issue occurred to me during that

Hollywood/Oscar flap back in February. Remember how Jesse was all over TV and radio, holding forth about racism in Hollywood, and how blacks don't get any recognition from the Motion Picture Academy? Even if he's right, I couldn't help wondering: Is this his job? Holding forth on things? Is he a *forth-holder*?

Why is it that if Jesse Jackson decides he wants to voice his opinion on something, the national press feels duty-bound to provide him a forum? Why would CNN give this guy his own show? I mean, it's not that I really dislike Jesse or anything. I just can't figure out what his qualifications are.

He's not really a politician. Technically, he's a "Shadow Senator," which is a title the visionaries in Washington, D.C., created in 1990. This "position" doesn't entitle Jesse to a vote in Congress, and he's not charged with representing anybody. Instead, he's supposed to lobby Congress for Washington, D.C. statehood (you can see how well he's done) (why do I sense the hand of Marion Barry in here?). This is almost as meaningless a post as Vice President (do you think they pay Jesse in "shadow dollars"?). Besides, I'm sure this "job" has nothing to do with why Jackson gets on TV so regularly — in fact, with the current condition of D.C., I'll bet "Shadow Senator" never even appears on Jesse's resume.*

And Jesse's not really a Reverend. Oh, I'm sure he meets all the *technical* requirements to be a man of the cloth, but where exactly is his church? Besides, how many real Reverends do you know with CNN contracts?

---

* Actually, Jesse's tenure as Shadow Senator is about to expire, and he's indicated he's no longer interested in the post. After all, he's been waiting for a chance to use all those frequent flyer miles.

He's certainly not an entertainer. I've watched his CNN show — 'nuff said there (just because he's a rhyming black guy doesn't make Jesse as inherently fascinating as, let's say, Nipsey Russell).

So what the heck is this guy? Is he just a professional activist? Is there such a thing? Can one make a living at it? One thing's for sure — whatever it is he does, he's been doing it a long time. It must be a *steady* job.

So I decided I would look into all this — and at the same time, see just how responsive our "elected public servants" are when a constituent actually wants to ask them something.

HELLO, IT'S ME AGAIN ...

None of the magazine or newspaper articles I went to seemed to have any more information on this mystery than I had, so I decided my best move would be to go right to the source. I called the Rainbow Coalition, the Washington-based organization Jesse founded in 1984. I figured they must be the people funding Jesse when he jets off to wherever the current racial flash point is. (See what I mean? What kind of job is this? Doesn't he have to punch in somewhere?). I reasoned if anybody knows what Jesse's job title is, it must be the Rainbow Coalition (of course, that then raises the question as to what exactly the Rainbow Coalition does, and who gives them the money to give to Jackson, but bear with me here).

I first spoke with whom I assume was the switchboard operator. She put me on hold for a few minutes, during which I was relieved to be treated to muzak rather than Jesse Jackson's greatest hits or something. When she came back, I asked to be connected to the Public Relations Department.

She transferred me to the voice mail of a woman whose tape identified her as "press secretary." I left a pretty detailed message on the voice mail, explaining how I had some very basic questions about the Rainbow Coalition, its funding, Jesse Jackson's activities, and so on (I used a sweet, accommodating voice, and said it would only take a few moments).

I never heard from her, so I tried again the next day. This time I actually left just my name and number, trying to spark her interest and trick her into calling. Same result. (These are the tactics that made my social life so legendary in high school).

My last attempt was to page her (she has her page number on her voice mail). I figured this had to work, because she wouldn't recognize my number; for all she knew, it could have been Denzel Washington calling to take her to a premiere or something. Same result. Now that's public relations, I thought.*

Oookay, back to the switchboard. I explained the problem I was having to the operator, and this time she recommended I speak to the "Political Director." She said he would be back in 15 minutes, and suggested I call then. I waited a half-hour just to be sure, then called. The switchboard operator told me he still hadn't returned, and now she wasn't sure when he'd be back — but would I like to speak to the Public Relations Department? "Sure!" I said. She then connected me — to that same woman's voice mail again. It was at this point that I began to suspect this switchboard operator might be sitting alone in an empty warehouse somewhere in Iowa.

---

* Perhaps she wasn't returning press calls because a recent issue of *The American Spectator* broke a story on Jesse demanding $400,000 to visit Angola (the Angolan government turned him down – can't imagine why).

SENATOR BLOW-OFF

I wasn't ready to give up. Did Helen give up on Odysseus? Stanley on Livingstone? The Captain on Tennille? My next plan was to call my Democratic Senator, Pat Moynihan. I figured he was a Democrat, hangs out in Washington, he must have met Jesse at some point. Besides, technically, as a New York Senator, Pat Moynihan works for me.

So I called his office in New York. The switchboard operator there (I swear, it sounded like the same woman) told me to call the Senator's office in Washington.

So I did. At first I got a recording that told me "all operators are busy, please hang on." Strangely, this time I *was* treated to Jesse Jackson's greatest hits (not really, but it would have been funny). Then a woman came on the line — the dreaded "switchboard operator." After hearing my request, she told me that I needed to speak with the "press secretary," but that he was not in. I left my number, but guess what? I'm still waiting.

Okay, enough of this crap, I decided. Maybe I was shooting a bit too high. I decided to just call my local Democratic Congressman, Gary Ackerman. I figured now with this guy, somebody's *got* to call me back. His office is right around here. I'll drive by and have my kids moon him if someone doesn't call.

Alright, I'll make this one short. I drove fast, my kids loved it, and I'm pretty sure nobody got my license plate.

MORE PHONE FUN: HOW I BLOW MY FIRST BIG INTERVIEW

I was paging through the newspaper shortly thereafter when I noticed that our friend Mr. Franken was again making the rounds of the liberal fund-raisers. Now, incredibly, when Franken plays these things, he recycles the identical jokes that he put in his book. No exaggeration, I must have seen or heard that "Having Al D'Amato chair an ethics committee ..." joke of his four or five times. And if he tells us again that Christine Whitman is a perfect cross between Charles and Di, Scotland Yard will probably booby-trap his cotton Dockers.

But that's not my point. See, there was something that had never occurred to me until I noticed Al in the paper again. If I wanted info about a prominent liberal like Jesse Jackson for my book, there's one guy I should have called from the start: Al Franken. After all, according to his own book, Franken spends a lot of time these days delighting his fellow Dems at these gala affairs (Dems that must have heard his jokes ten times by now). Franken *had* to sit next to Jesse at one point or another. Plus, I figured that if I could get Al on the phone, I could give him a chance to respond to some of the things I had already written for this book. Which only seemed fair.

I managed to get hold of Al's agent's office out in Los Angeles, and convinced them I was a fan and was writing an article on his book. Now, let me ask you something. Why is it that people who work for celebrities (or pseudo-celebrities, in this case) somehow feel that that makes them important as well? Suffice it to say that the woman in the agency that handles Franken is about as pleasant as a case of ringworm.

She is also utterly incompetent; after telling me she would talk to Al about an interview and then call me back with an interview date (thus assuring me plenty of lead time to prepare my questions), she blew me off and hung up. Imagine, then, my surprise when the phone rang a half-hour later, and Al Franken himself asked to speak to me.

Now in retrospect I should have expected this, as let's face it, Franken certainly knows free publicity when he sees it. But picture this. Here I am sitting at my kitchen table with dozens of old photos of Franken spread out in front of me; I was trying to pick the ugliest one for the "cheap shot photo" in Chapter 2 while actually talking to Al on the phone (I almost asked him his opinion). I swear, I was literally holding my nose to keep from giggling at one point.

In any case, I was very polite and expressed my thanks for his call, but explained to him that I had been mis-informed by his agent's office as to how this interview would work and did not have any questions ready. I asked if he could call back in ten minutes so I could prepare some good material for us to discuss. He said he was about to go out for a bit and would call when he returned; I told him he could call any time he wanted, no matter how late it got.

I guess I must have come across as rather small-time, as even though I waited up until 2 am, he never called back. I even put the phone next to my bed when I finally went to sleep, just in case Al came in late after clubbing with Panetta or someone. I called his agent again the next day, but Miss Charm was every bit as helpful the second time around. I mustn't sound like I work for *Entertainment Weekly* or *The Washington Post*.

I then gave a half-hearted try at Franken's publicist, which is some other breed of entertainment creature. Same luck. Maybe Al's finally busy writing himself a few new jokes, I thought.

So I was forced to write this book without Al Franken's assistance (which is a shame, because I really had a lot of trouble picking that "cheap shot" photo). Who knows? If he'd called me back, maybe this book would have been titled *Al Franken Is A Bucktoothed Friend of Mine.*

But that's not really my problem. Because my original dilemma continues to torment me, night and day. The Rainbow Coalition has failed me, the government has failed me, Al Franken has failed me. I've decided it's time to appeal to the general public, to take my quest to the streets. Can anybody out there help me? Does anyone really know?

Just what the heck does Jesse Jackson actually *do* for a living?

And do you think they're hiring?

24

DOES AL FRANKEN REALLY HAVE BUCKTEETH?

y publisher called in a panic yesterday and explained to me that in order to publish this book he needs to fill out something called an "ABI form," so that the book can be listed in some important catalog. I told him "lotsa luck" and being a good

Catholic, offered to make a novena for him.

After explaining to me that he was Jewish and had no clue what a novena was (he thought it was a skin cream or something — I explained to him how it's the sacred Catholic square dance), he told me he needed the official title of the book ASAP, and to stop screwing around.

Now at that point I was not completely positive about the title, because, in all honesty, I wasn't totally sure Al Franken really had buckteeth. When I first proposed the title to my wife, she laughed and said, "yeah, that's perfect, he does have buckteeth." While an immediate positive response like that would usually alleviate all my fears, I should point out that before this current project my wife backed me one hundred percent on a scheme to corner the Albanian joy-buzzer market. So I figured before I could give my publisher the final title, I needed to independently confirm Al's woodchuck incisors.

I trudged into Manhattan and started going through the files of every possible photo service. After about four hours of looking at old *Saturday Night Live* photos (saw some *electric* photos of Chevy), I concluded it's not so much that Al has buckteeth, it's that he has an overbite like a garden hoe (yes, if you're wondering, the cover is a tad "enhanced"). But what the hell, I decided, that's good enough to call him bucktoothed, especially when "moron" seemed to have such ... élan.

Besides, *Al Franken Is A Four-Eyed Shitbird* just wouldn't fit on the cover.

25

AN OPEN LETTER TO JANET RENO

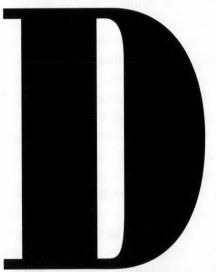ear Ms. Reno,

As I write this, the F.B.I. is involved in another standoff situation with a militia group, this one with the so-called "Freemen" of Montana. While at first much of the country seemed interested in this Freemen thing, once the number of days in the standoff began to exceed the length of the average Valerie Bertinelli miniseries, there has been a certain dropping off. With these militia situations becoming more and more common, I am writing to offer you a solution I've hit upon which I believe you'll find helpful in this and future standoffs.

First off, let me assure you that I realize these militia scenarios pose problems considerably more delicate than those the F.B.I. usually encounters. Aside from the fact that you generally face a group as well-armed as yourselves, there is the further problem that nobody is playing their assigned roles. According to the rules standardized for this sort of thing back in the Sixties and Seventies, these militia men are supposed to be radical left-wing, Symbionese Liberation Army/Weathermen types, and should have an heiress locked in a dungeon or something. Yet all these militia guys, we keep hearing, are actually radical *right-wingers*. Furthermore, there are elements in the current administration who are claiming that these militia encounters now make the *Democrats* the "law and order party" (I guess this could be true, if one accepts the idea that a few inbred militia losers who hate Bill Clinton and love playing G.I. Joe can somehow erase the Democrats' "turn-em loose" history). None of the usual standards seem to apply here; and so, confusion reigns.

Let me just say that I also appreciate that your people, facing intense scrutiny and mindful of other reactionary militia groups, fear a repeat of Ruby Ridge or Waco. In this most recent disturbance, they have therefore been tremendously patient with these Freemen characters. But the pace of these militia events has become entirely too dull. And so, as the current "law and order" Democratic administration clearly has little idea of how to handle these disturbances, and taking into account the concerns of your brave people in the field, I believe I have arrived at the solution.

Simply build a prison around the Freemen compound. As these militia encounters always take place in the middle of nowhere, there is generally plenty of land available for fences and towers and stuff, so this would work with any of these outlaw groups. Think about it. You've always got to have a whole gang of agents out at the scene anyway, watching and waiting and all. And I'm sure F.B.I. agents don't come cheap. So why not replace them with construction workers? Keep a few guys around with guns, so if the militia men see what's happening they can't start running away. Before you know it, you've got a whole new prison, and you haven't even had to spring for a trial or anything. Then when these militia guys finally do get wind of what's up and say, "Hey, okay, we'll come out now," you can tell them, "Oh, no. You had your chance." You can even put other prisoners in there with them — maybe some real mean ones. Look: They want to stay in there, and you want to put them in jail. You take my advice, everybody's happy.

Anyway, that's my idea, and I believe if you consider it carefully you'll find it'll work every time. Let's face it, these militia guys are not going to go away any time soon. So the next time this kind of thing happens, just slap up a couple of fences!

If you need to get hold of me to go over any of this further, you can contact me through my publisher, but I think the plan pretty much speaks for itself. There really aren't too many details. I only ask that if you use this idea, I get the credit for it. I don't want the "law and order" Democrats trying to claim this too, okay? Good luck.

26

WHY *STUART SAVES HIS FAMILY* IS THE WORST MOVIE EVER MADE

t started, I guess, way-back-when with Chevy. Even though it has now become conventional wisdom that Chevy Chase is essentially a loser, at the time people still had high hopes for anything *Saturday Night Live* touched. But then the films started coming, those awful, awful films, and we knew something had gone horribly wrong.

I mean, *Modern Problems* was one thing. But was *Oh, Heavenly Dog* really necessary? Did Chevy need the money that badly? Couldn't he have gone on *Match Game* or something? Even returning to *Saturday Night* would have been better than *Under the Rainbow* or *Deal of the Century* (or *Cops and Robbersons* or *Memoirs of an Invisible Man* or *Funny Farm* or *Nothing But Trouble* ...).

But by then Belushi and Aykroyd had taken over, and things looked good again. First came *Animal House*, and then *The Blues Brothers*, another step in the right direction. I was a kid, I loved those films, knew every line, and so did all my friends. And with *Stripes* and *Meatballs*, it looked like Bill Murray was going to come through for us, too. But then John died, and things began to go awry for good. Eventually even Aykroyd ended up doing *My Stepmother Is An Alien* and *Dr. Detroit*. Maybe it was better that John went before he ended up in *Dr. Detroit*, know what I mean?

Since then, of course, it's gotten even worse. I mean, I don't expect an *Animal House* right out of the box every time, I really don't, and I don't think the American public does, either. We're reasonable, we understand that sometimes a good idea can go south due to any number of uncontrollable factors.

But for a good while now, the endless stream of *Saturday Night Live* spinoff films that have been dropped on us has been like standing under a shit spigot. I mean, let's forget about Eddie Murphy's missteps, or the films of Mr. Joe Piscopo. Eddie outgrew SNL a long time ago, and I'm not sure what's become of Piscopo, I think he runs a gym out in Jersey with his baby-sitter or something. Let's just consider some of the recent blockbusters we have SNL members to thank for. Ready?

Billy Madison, It's Pat, Tommy Boy, The Coneheads, Happy Gilmore, Scrooged, Black Sheep, The Great Outdoors, Clifford, CB4, Airheads, So I Married An Axe Murderer, Exit to Eden, Celtic Pride, Opportunity Knocks, Man of the House ...

Good lord — let's stop there. Quite a roster, huh? Like the '93 Mets. But as bad as that is, as horrific as those films have been — sweet Jesus, this Stuart movie.

I only rented *Stuart Saves His Family* (hereinafter, *Viewer Save Your Money*) because I had to in order to write this chapter (even I was savvy enough to ignore SNL spin-offs after experiencing the dark comic genius that is Adam Sandler). But despite the voluminous trepidations I brought to this flick, Franken managed to outgun me. With this movie, Al Franken becomes the Michael Jordan of not funny. You think it's just me? Let's check in with a few other reviewers then, shall we?

Anti-affirmation for Stuart: You're NOT good enough, you're NOT smart enough, and doggone it, PEOPLE ARE GOING TO WALK OUT ON YOUR MOVIE! Al Franken's *Stuart Saves His Family* was a true jolt, one of the worst movies in many a year.
— *San Diego Union Tribune*

Hello, my name is Steve M., and I'm a recovering film critic. Thanks for letting me share. I'd like to start by making an amends in advance to Al Franken and his movie *Stuart Saves His Family*, which really reeks.
— *The Atlanta Journal and Constitution*

Stuart Saves His Family is 97 minutes more of Stuart Smalley than you want to see. Considering that the film is 98 minutes long, this is not a good ratio ... Do not go to this movie.
— *The San Francisco Examiner*

Is there a 12-step program for survivors of ill-advised *Saturday Night Live* movies? If not, there should be ...

Stuart Saves His Family is bad, stupid, and, doggone it, people are going to hate it.
— *The Toronto Star*

I wonder if Stuart can keep believing in himself after he sees the reviews for this movie. It's the first film of the year that's guaranteed a spot on my list of the worst movies of '95.
— *Gannett News Service*

And that's just the first few I pulled off the Nexis database (still a big Nexis fan, Al?).

Unaccountably, the only reviewers who seemed to find the *Stuart* movie even bearable were Siskel and Ebert, of all people. Now, I'm not going to rag on them for that, that's their opinion and that's not the purpose of this book. But I would like to ask both Roger and Gene one thing: *Just what fucking movie were you guys sitting through?* How could you actually send people to the theaters to see this film? Nice going, fellas. A Fat Man and Little Boy haven't been responsible for this much human misery since 1945.

What was so bad about it? For one thing, Al makes the classic mistake that many of the SNL members have made when bringing their characters over to the big screen. What worked for a couple of minutes on television is not necessarily going to be enough to sustain a full-length movie (see: *It's Pat, Coneheads*, etc.). Al decided he would solve this by fleshing out the Stuart character, by giving us Stu's family life and his poignant, serious side.

His *serious* side?

Yep. There is a point in this movie when it dawns on the viewer that Franken (the sole author of the script, incidentally) wants us to take Stuart *seriously*, that the film is trying to slip some "social commentary" by us when we least expect it. In Stuart's 12-step programs and his relentlessly dysfunctional family, Franken attempts to show us that, hey, humor is humor, but some things just aren't to be joked about. You can almost hear him in the background, intoning, "Yeah, funny is funny, but life's put me through some heavy changes, my friend. There's a point where the jokes just have to stop." It is at this juncture that I began to look around the room for the hidden camera. I mean, was this for real?

But it goes beyond that. It goes beyond the fact that I've read cereal boxes that were better scripted than this, and that the whole thing was probably a tax write-off for Lorne Michaels anyway. See, like I've already said, I grew up with *Saturday Night Live*, a show that Al wrote for. *Saturday Night* was a definite part of my generation's youth, a youth which hadn't felt so far gone to me, really. But with this movie, I had to consider the distance that's been traveled. This movie was so bad, it forced me to face my own mortality. Because if I gauge my age by the distance between *Stuart* and the old *Saturday Night Live* films, the *Animal Houses* and *Blues Brothers* — then I must have one foot in the grave. And *Stuart* put it there. For my generation, this is more than a bad film; it is a watershed event, a generational menopause. *Stuart Saves His Family* is cinematic prostate cancer.

Of course, it sucks for other generations, too. Hey — it sucks for all ages! And that's why it's the worst movie ever made.

27

OUR LEGAL SYSTEM EXAMINED

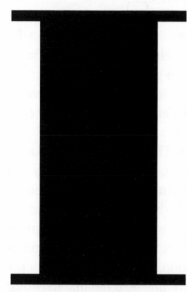 don't know why I'm even bothering to write this. See, this was supposed to be a chapter on the need for reform in the American legal system, with various recommendations on how to renew our faith in it during this post-O.J. age. I'd researched it, read up on it, even conducted an informal poll. But now I'm not even going to bother. Screw it.

Because it finally happened, like everyone always said it would. I finally got mugged.

You want to know why we need legal reform? Listen to this. I was coming home on the subway, which I take to another train, which takes me to a station, where I pick up my car and then drive home. This series of connections has taken years off my life, and has, I've been told, invested my face with the sort of permanent wince best associated with John Bobbitt. I've also been told I would someday regret continuing to ride the subway; but where is a white-collar worker, who works in Manhattan and has a family, going to live? The upper West Side? I can't even afford the doughnuts in Franken's neighborhood.

Anyway, it's probably my own fault. I got off a bit late, and instead of going right home, I headed downtown for some shopping. My sister and Andre the liberal have moved into a new house, and I wanted to get them a housewarming present. There are all sorts of good bargains to be had in Chinatown, so I went down to Canal Street and got them a nice coffee maker.

Then I was hungry, so I dipped into the Hong-Fat Noodle Company for a little sesame chicken, which I must say was right on the money. Anyway, by the time I got back uptown and caught my train for home, rush hour was long over, and to make a long story short, there were only a few people in my car, which was near the end of the train. So a guy got on and right before the next stop, he stuck a sharpened screwdriver in my face. He then informed me that he would be relieving me of various worldly possessions he felt I could safely do without.

And you know what the little thief got? Aside from the coffee maker, and the leftover sesame chicken, he got my briefcase. And in my briefcase was my laptop. And on my laptop was: the only existing version of the rough draft for my book.

Anyway, I made out a report at the police station, but even the cops told me not to hold out much hope. This is a common thing in Fun City nowadays.

So how about that? I guess that's the end of the book —

I don't think I've got the heart to go slogging through the whole thing again. I probably wouldn't make the deadline anyway.

And *that's* why I'm not bothering to examine the legal system.

I'll bet the little bastard was a Democrat.

Incredible news — I got my laptop back! The system does work sometimes! The amazing details follow.

Apparently, the guy who robbed me has made quite a habit of this. So just by luck, a cop car was cruising by a store front that was suspected of being a "fence" for stolen goods. Anyway, my guy was out in front of this place, about to unload a whole cache of stuff from the back seat of his car. One look at the cop car, and the guy takes off running.

The cops check the guy's car, and when they open up the bags they find all sorts of suspicious-looking stuff, computers and watches and stuff. So one of the cops jumps back in his car and takes off after the guy, and he nails him. And it turns out that one of the items in the crook's car was — my laptop!

So today I had to go down to the station and identify the suspect — and sure enough, it was him. The dope even said hello to me. Can you believe that? I guess it wasn't his stellar SAT scores that landed him in his particular line of work.

Anyway, the cops kept the laptop, it's evidence and all that, but I'll get it back in plenty of time to make deadline.

The book is back on track, and the crook is going to jail! I finally get a break. God loves a Republican!

The system sucks.
I got a call yesterday from the cops telling me I could go

down to the station and pick up my laptop, they don't need it anymore. I figured that meant they had already had the trial or the guy had taken a plea or whatever. So while I was there I told the cop that they do great work, and fast, too — it's only been a couple of weeks since I was mugged.

And you know what the cop told me? He told me they didn't need the laptop anymore because the guy *got off*. Is that incredible? Apparently, the guy's lawyer petitioned the judge to throw the whole thing out, because he said the cops did not have "reasonable suspicion" to go through the crook's bags. It was "illegal search and seizure," a technicality.

Reasonable suspicion? The guy is standing in front of a fencing operation, and bolts like a jackrabbit when he sees the cop car — and they didn't have reasonable suspicion to check his bags? What were they supposed to think, the guy was late for work? Boy, was this cop pissed.

Anyway, the judge ruled that it was "reasonable" for this kid to take off when he saw the cops, as in that neighborhood, it is "reasonable" to fear the police — so they had no right to check his bags. I wonder if this judge would find it *reasonable* if I lost one of my size elevens in his crack. I doubt he'd find this whole thing reasonable in *his* neighborhood (the upper West Side or some *reasonable* facsimile, no doubt).

So this character is out there walking around somewhere, replete with screwdriver. For the first time in my life, I understand why people actually move to places like Utah.

Anyway, at least I got the book back — otherwise, you wouldn't be reading this. That's *something*, at least.

Guess what? It turns out the system *does* work. Oh yeah, it works. It works real great. If you're a *criminal*, it works just friggin' *perfect.*

Because that guy? The guy that stole my laptop? The little sonofabitch is suing me.

Are you seated? Comfortable? Good, that's nice. You want to hear a little story?

It turns out that after he got off, my friend went home and went to sleep. And the next morning when he woke up, he made himself a lovely fresh pot of coffee. That's right. With my coffee maker.

Apparently, the little bastard needed one, so he kept the coffee maker he took from me rather than trying to fence it. And now he says that the coffee maker makes the coffee too hot, and so when he picked up the pot, he dropped it and spilled some on his leg.

And so this little mercenary and his lawyer are now claiming that, because he was never convicted of a crime, and because he got the coffee maker from me, he's entitled to $57 million of my money for his "terrible suffering." Which, of course, is money I happen to have on me, so there's no problem there.

I would very much like to kill this guy, slowly and while inflicting maximum agony. Maybe something with wire or a trimming shears. Then I take care of the lawyer.

What I've done instead, however, is hire Andre to try to bail me out of this whole mess. He says he'll do it for the price of a new coffee maker if I plug his political action committee in my book, but I think he was just joking.*

Yeah, this is some great system we have. You think it's too late to go to law school?

---

* **Democrats for Sloths** can be reached at (1-900) 4-SLOTHS. They are a "progressive political party dedicated to correcting the abuse that was brutally directed against these wonderful quadrupeds during the fascist regimes of Ronald Reagan and George Bush." I cannot recommend them highly enough.

28

LIBERALS —
THEY FEEL YOUR PAIN

ou know, liberals do have certain talents, and one of the things they do particularly well is guilt. Not only do liberals manage to feel guilty over just about anything they can, they are more than willing to share that guilt with you, whether you're interested in sharing it or not. You want proof? They even got to me.

Writing this book, I've occasionally had pangs of conscience about making certain jokes. True, the Democrats are an irritating bunch, and seem to take a rather "freewheeling" approach to reality as we know it. But they're still people, still (technically) my fellow Americans. "I suppose they must mean well," I have sometimes found myself thinking. "Do they really deserve to have their noses rubbed in it so blatantly?"

Well you know what? I think they do. And you know why? Because despite all that guilt, despite all that *empathizing* and *commiseration*, despite how much they *feel my pain*, there's one basic fact that shows what phonies they can really be. Talk to them, deal with them a bit, challenge them at all, and they reveal this simple fact: *Nobody is nastier than a liberal scorned.*

I know what you might be thinking. You might be saying to yourself, "Yes, liberals are thick, pious, out-of-touch, smug — just some of the qualities that make them so wonderful to carpool with. But I never thought of them as *nasty*." Well, tell you what, let's try a little experiment. Consider: Where does liberalism in America most commonly flourish? Answer: In the politics of the Democratic Party, and in the media. So let's take the most liberal person in American politics and the most powerful liberal in American media, and see just how *compassionate* they really are. Fair enough?

BARNEY FRANK — STATESMAN, LIBERAL, NASTY BASTARD

It is generally conceded that of the many liberal Democrats clogging things up on the Hill, Barney's the furthest left of all of them. As, in his words, "a left-handed gay Jew," Barney has had to put up with intolerance his whole life; you would think by now Barney might be able to muster a little tolerance himself. Barney Frank, however, seems to be above that. Or to the left of it, you might say.

In a recent interview in *The New York Times*, Frank had this to say when asked if he hated Newt Gingrich: "Oh yeah, I despise Gingrich ..." Charming. Now, that may be the case — but can you imagine Gingrich saying the same thing publicly? That he *hates* Barney Frank? Hey Barney, do you know what a *hate* group is? Barney then goes on to admit to using the threat of "outing" gay Republicans in order to influence policy on the hill, a little legislative blackmail worthy of J. Edgar himself. Sweet, huh?

But it's for Bob Dole that Frank saves his most heartwarming empathy. After calling Dole "stupid," Frank is then asked to comment on Dole's professed regret over a misunderstanding the Republican Presidential candidate had with a group of gay supporters. "Well, I'm sure Mussolini, if we could ask him, would regret World War II," Frank replies. Why in God's name does Frank bring up Mussolini, of all people? Because this abominable crack essentially boils down to: "Oh, you're sorry, Dole? Well, then I guess Mussolini is real sorry about your arm, too." Dole, you'll recall, was badly wounded in Italy during World War II, and has not had the use of his right arm since.

Barney Frank — sometimes, you can just love *too* much.

TED TURNER — SOUTHERN-FRIED HUMP

Ted Turner is another of the prominent liberals I occasionally felt guilty about haranguing. I mean, despite the Jane Fonda thing, he can't be all bad. For instance, in 1990, Ted was voted "Humanist of the Year" by the American Humanist Association, an honor Turner shares with the likes of Andrei Sakharov and Jonas Salk. That's heavy company.

Ted has even come up with a list of ten "voluntary initiatives" to help change the world for the better. Number one is, "I promise to have love and respect for planet Earth and living things thereon, especially my fellow species humankind." Number two is nice, too: "I promise to treat all persons with dignity, respect and friendliness." Who could argue with that?

Now, of all the hard-core liberals in America's media, Ted is arguably the most powerful. His ownership of CNN alone probably qualifies him for this, never mind his other television stations and holdings. The guy is practically unchallenged. Which is a good thing, because when Ted Turner is challenged, watch out. When he doesn't get his way, Ted has probably said more downright nasty things about people than Marge Schott on a three-day bender. And I'm not talking about one-on-one nasty, although he's probably just as endearing in person. I'm talking about insulting or demeaning whole races of people. And somehow, he gets away with it because he's supposed to be such an "eccentric" and such a "good guy at heart." He's just a *cute* little 'ol bigot, is all.

Take his recent remarks about wanting to buy one of the major commercial television networks. The guy already owns CNN, TNT, TBS, Turner Classic Movies, The Cartoon Channel, and God knows what else. But because nobody will sell him CBS, NBC, or ABC, the mainstream commercial networks, he says, "I feel like those Jewish people in Germany in 1942. I know exactly what it is to be rounded up and herded out and sent to the east somewhere, resettled." Let me get this straight, Ted — the five TV networks you own aren't enough for you, and so now you're comparing yourself to a fucking *Holocaust victim*?

Ted went on to deplore the violence on television, and

then to say, "We've never made a movie as gratuitously violent as 'Pulp Fiction'... But maybe we will. If we do, I'll feel bad about it." Oh, thank God! At least he's got the guilt working. This guy wants another TV station? Give him a TV dinner and tell him to go watch *Barbarella* for the fortieth time.

Alright, maybe those remarks weren't completely nasty, maybe they were just insensitive and tremendously ignorant. But Ted's covered a few other groups too. He opines that Italians would "rather be involved in crime and just making wine and having a good time." Saw that in a movie, huh Ted? On Christians: "Christianity is a religion for losers." Indubitably. On an anti-abortion group: "We'll give the bozos a chance to talk. They look like idiots anyway." To a British reporter, following an English yacht race in which 15 sailors died: "You ought to be grateful for storms like that or you'd all be speaking Spanish" (referring to the ill-fated Spanish Armada).

Hey Ted, what happened to voluntary initiatives one and two?! Jeez, I hope none of the folks over at the "American Humanist Association" heard any of these cracks. Oh well. At least he supports the spotted owl. That's the important thing.

Alright then, let's forget those two big shot Democrats — maybe they haven't been getting enough bran in their diets or something. Let's just jump to the nearest liberal at hand. Al Franken's got a lovely little track record on this. Now, forget about the jokes he's written on *Saturday Night Live* or some of the nasty stuff he said in that book of his (I guess he's allowed to be purposely rude right to Al D'Amato and Newt Gingrich's faces. He's a crusading liberal comedian, get it? He's on a *mission*). Alright, forget all that. You want proof that the more liberals talk about compassion, the more

willing they are to twist the blade in anyone they don't like?
On page 216 of his book, Franken relates this bit:

> And while we're on Limbaugh and the subject of "fair
> mean" vs. "unfair mean," let's go back to 1993. On his TV
> show he put up a picture of Socks, the cat, and said, "Did
> you know there's a White House dog?" Then he put up a
> picture of 13-year-old Chelsea Clinton. But you know, she
> asked for it.

Franken finds the joke out of line. Fair enough. But then,
at the recent White House Correspondents Association
dinner in New York, Franken went on to tell a joke playing
off of Newt Gingrich's well-publicized statement about
women being unsuited for military combat because of their
menstrual cycle. And who was right in the crowd? Newt
Gingrich. And who was the "13-year old" that Franken used
as the subject of his menstrual joke? Newt Gingrich's
daughter.

But you know, she asked for it.

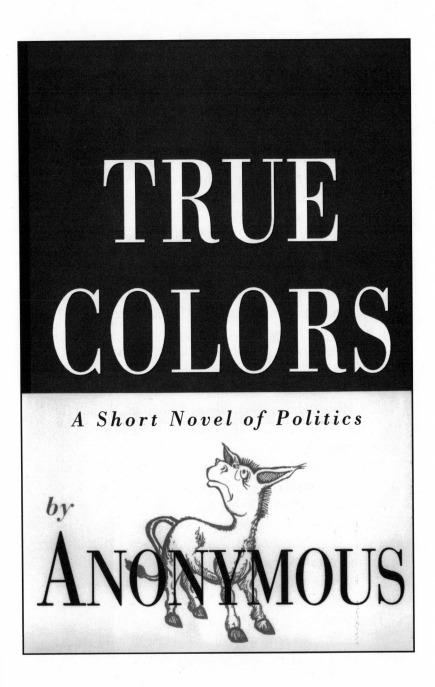

TRUE COLORS

A Short Novel of Politics

by

ANONYMOUS

I

He had that way of looking at you when he knew he'd let you down. The half-smile, wan and self-deprecating, conveying the requisite guilt. The voice a bit softer than usual, heavier, cut with *mea culpa*. But the posture was as confident as ever, the chin as high, the eyes as clear. It was forward-looking posture, the body language of a progressive. *Yes, I've let you down*, the whole picture said. *But we go on from here.*

"Is there any Yoo-hoo left in the fridge?" he grunted, pushing past me.

Of course; the last Yoo-hoo. I'd been saving it, had forgotten all about it. As always, he was faster than me.

Jack Stanton, President of the United States, came back into my office slurping chocolate Yoo-hoo. It was a tableau that said as much about American democracy as my complete set of "Constitutional Moments" commemorative jelly jars.

"So, Henry," he said. He always said that. He had this ... *way* of referring to me by my name. "What do you hear out in the swarm?"

"Well, sir, most of the press is back-burnering it. A few of the usual hornets have gone jugular, but that's par."

He didn't seem to be listening; I seemed to be telling him things he already knew, or wasn't concerned about. He was above these scandals, I suddenly realized; Jack Stanton breathed the rarefied air of ideals.

His eyes were focused somewhere over my shoulder. On the future, I guessed.

Then something hard hit me on the head, from behind. "Ow!" I said, as I remember it. What else could I say?

The air around me was suddenly dense with flying file

folders as I whirled around, knowing it would be *her*.

"You miserable asshole!" Susan Stanton screamed at her husband from the doorway. "You rotten sonofabitch! You fuck up as usual, and the press blames this whole thing on me!"

My head beginning to hemorrhage, I looked over to see if she'd gotten Jack too, to gauge his reaction. He was pulling himself up out of a crouch, his little half-smile intact. He'd ducked, of course.

Like I said, he was always faster than me.

II

"McTucker's gotta fall on his sword," Richard, our old campaign manager, was saying in his animated Louisiana twang. He was pacing as usual, his rail-thin frame all nervous tics and twitches. "We're gonna build us a fire wall, and McTucker's gonna fall on his sword and expire like a stuck hog." We were all looking at him. Y'knowhat-tamean?"

We were starting to. Jack sat at the head of the table, wearing his cashmere sweater, looking dignified and Presidential, very Jack Kennedy via-Hyannis Port. Susan sat next to him, her face gone stepford wife, staring chilly lasers around the room.

Across from me, sitting cunningly, was our special operative; Libby Holden, stealth digger. "YOU BET HE'LL FALL ON HIS SWORD," Libby barked in her coolest manner, lifting us out of our seats as her head swiveled like an apoplectic Stevie Wonder. "HE'LL FALL ON HIS SWORD OR I'LL SHOVE IT UP HIS DIMPLED ASS."

Typical private investigator, Libby. All nuance.

The Lightwater scandal had broken over us yesterday. Jack's old buddies from back home, the McTuckers, had just been convicted in the Lightwater land swindle, and the press was implying that Jack was involved (after all, *The Washington Post* did have copies of canceled checks totaling over a hundred thousand dollars made out to Jack from McTucker, all memoed "payoffs"). Some of the media ink had begun to stick; our damage-control team had assembled immediately.

Richard, ever the campaign manager, saw right to the crux. "If McTucker keeps his yap shut," he mused, his cheek twitching like a triphammer, "we ride this thing out. McTucker takes the bite, we spin the gestalt, and we quietly make sure McTucker's solvent for the rest of his natural life." His shoulders began to violently bounce now, like twin pistons.

A set of keys sailed past my head; Susan getting my attention. "Henry?" she said icily. "Opinion?"

"We say those checks were to a *different* Jack Stanton," I said, catching Richard's wave. "And McTucker swears to it. We say — "

"YOU BET YOUR GODDAMN ASS MCTUCKER SWEARS TO IT," Libby roared at the ceiling, her huge body bucking violently in her seat. "MCTUCKER SWEARS TO IT OR I'LL STRANGLE HIM WITH A GODDAMN EXTENSION CORD."

They were caught up in it now, Stanton believers again, excited by the promise of a new round of spin-doctoring. Richard was jerking around the room like some cretinous marionette, yelping "Koppel!" and "Brinkley!," and Libby went into her wookie howl (who knew then that the next day she would decide she desperately missed "New Coke" and so would take her own life?). *We might get out of this yet,* I thought.

But as I glanced at the head of the table, I noticed that Jack had slipped to the floor under his seat, and was sound asleep. I felt some doubt return.

III

The phone was ringing the way it did during campaigns; a series of short bursts, one after the other. The "campaign ring." I answered it.

"Hello?" It sounds gratuitous now, but at the time it seemed a noble gesture.

"Henry? Richard," the voice on the line said. I noticed it wasn't even light yet. What time was it?

"We got new problemas, chico. That's a factdoodle. We got muchas problemas," he said, as ever just shy of coherence. He sounded excited; I guessed the thorazine dart Susan had blow-gunned into his neck had finally worn off.

"What now?"

"A new thing, amigo. Turns out our man Jack got some White House doughboy to request a few files from the FBI. *Republican* files, tú sabes? Anyway, tomorrow's *Post* has it. Our culos couldn't be higher in the fryer."

Great. The Lightwater thing had finally been dying on the vine, the press having nowhere to go with it once Jack told them he'd been "a bit tired lately, and not really up to remembering details." But now they would eat us alive. "Where's Jack?" I asked him. "How's he holding up?"

"At the White House. And not too well. They were backing an 18-wheeler of Dunkin' Donuts up the drive when

I left." He paused. "This is muy malo, hombre. That is a jolly-roger bona-fide."

That was clear enough. "Somebody better tell Susan," I said.

"Sí. But I don't even know donde está."

So I figured. "What do you think we do?"

"No es una pregunta fácil. Y no me importa. Y'knowhattamean? Zài Shànghai de nà ge Meiguó yisheng yijing tuįìxiu le ma? Sharooo! Sharooo! Beghorra and sharooo! Y'hear? Y también, creo que estoy embarazada. Es increíble, no?"

It was. "Well, I'll find Susan," I said, trying to maintain perspective. "Shouldn't you get some rest?"

"Cómo está Usted? Muy bien, gracias. Y tú? Donde están los zapatos de la Señora Fernandez? Los zapatos de la Señora Fernandez están en la cocina. Cómo se llama su perro? Mi perro se llama — "

I hung up as Richard launched into "Eres Tú." I didn't have the heart to discuss campaign strategy now.

I rolled over in bed, watching her sleep, loving the curve of her neck, the throb of her carotid. And the special way she had of breathing: first in, then out. Then in. Then out. It was miraculous.

I decided I'd better wake her. "Susan," I said, gently shaking her shoulder. "Susan, wake up. I have some news."

She didn't take it well, I'm afraid. I needed eight stitches.

IV

I'd been in politics almost 15 years now, had gone to the good schools, worked with the quality people. I knew all the players, knew how the game worked. And despite what the papers said about me, about my youth, at 35, I was no rookie. I considered myself a seasoned pro.

And yet, as always, he still managed to surprise me.

He was focused, as focused and intense as I had ever seen him. "Henry, shoot me those Doritos, will you?" Jack said, his feet up on his desk. Even with his face and fingers covered with that yellow Doritos stuff, his dignity, his *Presidentialness*, remained total.

And so we sat in Jack Stanton's White House office, watching CNN, waiting for the final act to play itself out.

Susan was there, slightly preoccupied as she fired ninja stars at a picture of Jack taped to a dartboard. She was even good at that, I noticed. Practice.

The end was due at any moment. Jack's White House doughboy, Livingstein, was up on the TV screen now, filling it, getting ready to testify that Jack had ordered him to obtain the classified FBI files. They were calling it "Foldergate."

It was sad, a sadness I felt throughout my whole body. My colon ached. Yet I was proud of him, too. Jack was going to take the fall here, and hard. But he wasn't trying to duck it, wasn't trying to weasel by it. He was, again, the Jack Stanton I knew.

I was glad to be here with him. The rest of our team had proved their loyalty immediately, as I'd known they would. I estimated Richard's plane would be touching down in Kuala Lumpur about now. But Jack and I were together. It meant a lot.

Then, as we sat there waiting for the axe to fall, Jack did a very strange thing. He got up from his chair and began to sway a bit, humming softly. And then he began to dance.

It was something to see. He sashayed across the room

towards Susan, who had her back to him, and gave her a quick kiss on the neck; then he went into a little shuffle.

It was just a two-step, but to see it was to have it break your heart. How that man could soft shoe! Then he started into something else, a sort of free-form, interpretive jazz thing, featuring a lot of dramatic kicks and whirls. He danced for me, for Susan, for himself. He was dancing for us all.

He started singing too, a scat-Gregorian chant medley. I could feel the tears starting to come.

Susan stopped him. *"What the hell are you so happy about, you incredible jackass?"* she said. Just what was she implying?

It was then that Craig Livingstein's voice sprang from the TV, as if on cue. "I am resigning my position as White House security chief," he said solemnly. "As for any other questions this committee might have, may I just say that strangely, I have no recollection of anything before waking up this morning."

I looked at Jack. What was this?

He slid a file folder across his desk at me. "Take a look," he said casually. "But brace yourself."

Inside the folder were ... *things*. Things that made me question my life, my humanity. That made me question the fate of mankind, adrift in a godless cosmos. I suddenly felt as if I'd stubbed my toe, or worse. The room began to spin. I fell back into a chair.

"That's right," Jack said, straightening his tie. The 2-step had left him a bit disheveled, red-faced and sweaty; he was giving off a scent like an overheated musk ox. "Those are all genuine photographs. Livingstein in a pair of Speedos. They were taken on a beach in Barbados last year by a National Geographic photographer." I gulped for air; it had been too horrible to contemplate.

Jack saw the look on my face. "Yeah, Livingstein thought so too," he said. "All Richard had to say to him was 'Geraldo,' and Livingstein cut the deal on the spot."

My head was still swimming; my entire psychic landscape had just shifted beneath my feet, or something. How could Jack do this?

As usual, he knew what I was thinking. "This is politics, Henry," he said, his eyes a sudden Greek tragedy. "You're still with us, aren't you?"

I looked away, up at the TV screen, where Craig Livingstein had put his hands over his ears and was yodeling in order to avoid hearing the Committee's questions. I didn't blame him.

"Honey, could you be a sweetheart and get me and Henry something to drink?" Jack suddenly said, flashing her a smile, a number four I think, the warm domestic one. She hocked a looie in his direction, but did leave the room.

"Look, Henry," Jack said. There he was again, calling me by my name. The guy knew all the tricks. "You've got to stay on. Please. We need you. Although I'm not exactly sure what it is you do. But come on. I'm begging you."

He gave me that look then, that same *I've let you down but we go on* look. This time, though, it spoke to me of other things. It spoke of my future, of changes, of a new beginning for a nation. It spoke of White House receptions, Caribbean vacations, early retirement. A consulting firm in Arlington. A few divorces. A debilitating stroke, incontinence, a sparsely attended funeral. A bitter estate battle. How he got all this into one slightly raised eyebrow amazed me.

Susan came back into the room, holding a couple of bottles. "How about a Yoo-hoo, Henry?" Jack said to me, his voice sincere.

I let it hang in the air a moment. I was looking at Jack when I answered.

"Yes," I told him, as his mouth curled in a little smile. "Yes, I think I would like a Yoo-hoo."

It just missed my head. Looking back at Jack, I saw he was already down, taking cover behind his desk.

As I said, he was always faster than me.

THE END

30

TRACKING AN NEA GRANT

f you're completely befuddled as to what that last chapter was, don't start pricing therapists. That was just my take on *Primary Colors*, this year's bestselling political novel. If you haven't read it, the novel follows the ascent of a character clearly based on Bill Clinton and his cohorts, and it's been the talk of Washington for awhile now (roughly until the figure of Craig Livingstone emerged from the shadows to startle us all). Anyway, while *Primary Colors* is a terrific read, I felt the anonymous author (rumored to be *Newsweek*'s Joe Klein) had clearly neglected a few key moments from the inspiring Bill Clinton saga.

Alright, enough of that, I'm not getting any royalties

from *Primary Colors*. New issue: the National Endowment for the Arts (the NEA).

Now, the question of whether or not the government should provide money for funding the arts is, believe it or not, one I find quite complicated. True, a great deal of the money granted by the NEA is wasted on the sort of vanity projects most of us were supposed to outgrow by junior high. And that money could be put to better use in more utilitarian areas of public funding, like (gasp) welfare.

On the other hand, as one of the richest nations in history, do we really want our artistic legacy to rest with Chuck Norris? Yes, I know, the "fine arts" are as strong a bastion of ultra-liberalism as there exists in America. And yes, many of the "artists" take obscene sums of money and then produce works like "Opus #6: My Toaster in D-Minor" or a painting that looks like it was done by an orangutan with Tourette's.

But one of the measures of a civilization will always be the eternal things that it leaves behind, the things of beauty or insight that last, the Confucian Analects or Homer's dramas or Beethoven's symphonies. Sure, we've had Scott Fitzgerald and Charlie Chaplin and Chuck Berry (guys who I — sincerely — believe will be globally remembered as long as Beethoven), and of course there have been others; but in terms of our worldwide influence, it seems like there has to be better people for us to constantly throw the word "genius" at than Prince, or whatever he's called these days.

Surprisingly, the group who seems to have gotten this whole NEA thing in the right perspective is the ACLU. Their position is quite logical: If the government wants to fund the arts, it cannot then dictate in any way what sort of art grant-recipients produce. Otherwise, don't fund the arts.

After much head-holding and lip-chewing, I'm inclined to wince and agree. Despite where some of the money ends up.

THE BIG NIGHT. Karen begins her performance by reading selections from a collection of 16th Century Finnish whaling poems.

Karen then wraps herself in the American flag and invites the crowd onstage to urinate on her.

Among the crowd of seven, including Karen's parents and her Tasmanian boyfriend, there are no takers.

Encouraged by the overwhelming response to her art, Karen applies for another grant to take her "work-in-progress" on the road.

Next stop: Paris!

End

31
IT TAKES A DEMOCRAT

**It Takes A Village
(And Other Lessons
Children Teach Us)**
*by Hillary Rodham Clinton
318 pp. Simon & Schuster:
$20.00*

nfortunately for Hillary, what it took was a *ghostwriter* to complete her book. And a very dull ghostwriter at that. I mean, televised-golf dull. Al Gore-dull.

I'm talking world-class dull. Who knew Eleanor Roosevelt was this boring?

You want me to sum this book up for you?

"We should do more for our children."

That, believe me, says as much as all 318 pages of Hillary's book. If conciseness is a requisite of good writing, I just beat Hillary's ghostwriter by over 317 pages (get the Guinness people on the phone).

Now, you knew I wasn't going to like Hillary's book (in all honesty, so did I). I did, however, give more credit to whatever focus group developed "The Book Project" for the Democrats and the First Lady. I mean, who was in charge of the "make-it-interesting" unit? Panetta? *It Takes A Village* is so numbingly repetitive, I only managed to read the first 18 pages. Then I read the last 18 pages, just to pretend I read the whole book. The rest, I just sort of skimmed. But, you know, I could tell it sucked. It even skimmed dull.

If you do manage to read some of this book, and actually plod through what has to be some sort of a record for platitudes-per-page ratio, Hillary will reward you with her homespun little ideas about dealing with children (her ghostnanny must have dictated them to her ghostwriter). In fact, the book is so packed with these little ideas and sayings that I began to actually get concerned I was doing everything wrong, and that my kids were going to grow up like Macaulay Culkin.

But when I put the book down to get my note pad, I glanced at the back cover and realized something with relief. I was reading the wrong how-to book! You see, the back cover has a picture of Hillary surrounded by ten little kids; three boys and seven girls, but luckily for me, *no white males*. And I have two boys! White boys! Hillary, thank God, must have intended this book only to apply to girls and minority boys. No wonder the book seemed dull to me!

You know what else is way off here? The title. Why an African proverb? I'm sure Hillary loved the homey, caring connotation the title has, thought it would sell books and impress reviewers. But I don't think she realized that the title connotes the fact that in Africa these days, it also takes a village to mutilate young girls' sex organs; it takes a village to sell 12-year-olds into prostitution; it takes a village to possess the highest infant mortality rate of any continent; and it takes a village to spread AIDS and the Ebola virus like wildfire. It's more than sad. It's a *tragic* state of affairs in Africa right now. You think these are really the villages Hillary wanted it to take?

Anyway, along with the "we're all responsible" drum that the book beats incessantly, Hillary also dwells on the "government should take more responsibility in raising children" theme (actually, I was happy to read this, as next time I'm a little tired and the baby needs changing, I think I'll phone my assemblyman). This "government-as-nurturer" aspect of the book is, of course, no accident, which brings up what is really wrong with this hollow-but-harmless work.

Does whoever put this book together really think we're that stupid? Are we not supposed to notice this election year family-values campaign Hillary has suddenly launched? Being married to the Warren Beatty of politics as she is, and with the Republicans having clear precedence over the family-values issue, I guess the Dems felt they better do something. But this saccharine book, in combination with her sudden (and potentially dangerous) desire to have another child at 49 years of age, is the most transparent public-relations ploy since O.J. vowed to find the real killers (of course, if she crosses me up and actually manages to produce a child, I'm going to look awfully foolish). It's been like, what, 14 years since Chelsea? And *now* Hillary's hell-bent for offspring?

My prediction is that the Clintons will neither have another child, nor will they adopt one, as Hillary has also suggested (although they would probably adopt a *walrus* if it would guarantee them another term). Adopting a child raises all sorts of voter-demographic problems for the Dems. What color/ethnicity should the kid be? How old? Boy or girl? A foreign baby or an American? I don't really believe the Democrats want to get into all of this. Hillary is just floating the idea to see if any votes stick to it.

Which makes this, as a wise reviewer once said, "not a book to be tossed aside lightly. It should be thrown with great force."

32

BILL CLINTON: CHALLENGED ON ALL SIDES

was reading today about the financial boondoggle known as Whitewater (a task comparable to reading a computer manual in Norwegian, though slightly less exciting). The pundits seem to think the convictions of a couple of Clinton's buddies in connection with Whitewater spells more trouble for

Clinton's sterling reputation, which as of this writing is hovering around Joey Buttafuoco levels.

I couldn't help wondering, with all the liabilities Clinton has as a candidate, whether he was the best the Democrats could put forward. We heard so much about all the Republican candidates in New Hampshire, but nothing of the other Democrats on the ballot. Is it just a given these days that nobody can successfully challenge an incumbent President? (Teddy Kennedy beat incumbent Carter in some key primaries in 1980; and remember Eugene McCarthy? He essentially drove incumbent LBJ out of the race in 1968). Now, if there is one thing I remember from Mrs. Gordon's fifth-grade Civics class, it's that virtually anyone can run for President (that, and that Patrick McNally could drink milk through his ears). So, I decided to see if anyone actually did challenge Clinton in New Hampshire.

Believe it or not, this could have been important. For instance, what if the printer in New Hampshire had forgotten to include the name "Clinton" on the ballot? (Believe it or not, it actually appeared as just "Bill" — how nauseating is that?). My God! Do you realize that would have made Pat Paulsen the winner of the most important primary in the country?

Pat Paulsen, in case you don't remember, is the comic of *Smothers Brothers* "fame" who has been running mock Presidential campaigns since the 1960s. He actually wound up second in this year's New Hampshire Democratic primary, with 921 votes (hey, that actually registers as 1% of the vote! Clinton got 95% with 76,754 votes). But Paulsen's campaign was a joke (I think ... I *hope*); I think people vote for him just so they can laugh about it later with their buddies (my theory on how Clinton won in '92). But what about the other candidates? Who were these brave

Democrats the press was keeping from us? We have a right to know!

Well, let's see, there was Osie Thorpe from Washington, D.C. He lost the last D.C. Mayoral race to Marion Barry in 1994. No, he never had a chance in New Hampshire — too radical. I mean, he called the *dashiki-clad* Marion Barry an "Uncle Tom." Besides, anyone who couldn't beat that basket-case Barry should just go back to the night shift at Denny's.

How about Heather Harder from Indiana? Nah, she claims to communicate with other dimensions ... she was un-electable from the get-go (although that didn't seem to hurt Jerry Brown). Hmm, there must have been someone else worthwhile. Bruce Daniels? He says he smoked pot (he even inhaled) *and* he avoided the draft. Hey, maybe we're onto something here! Nah, he lives in Canada, I'm not even sure that's legal. Besides, one Bill Clinton is enough.

How about Caroline Killen from Flagstaff? A 70-year-old ex-nun whose platform was the legalization of marijuana. Let's see, Caroline, a lesbian, was busted in 1987 for urinating in public, and she now lives in a tent which also serves as campaign headquarters. Nah, I don't think so. I mean the woman lives in a tent, but she's forking-over $1,000 to enter a primary — bad on financial issues.

Alright, he wasn't the most interesting, but I guess "Bill" probably *was* the Democrat's best choice ... at least Clinton hasn't urinated in public (Bill that is, not Roger).

You know what, though? We don't hear enough about these alternative candidates. Because I should point out that the Democrats don't have a monopoly on this particular breed of political nonconformist.

For instance, what about Lyndon LaRouche, who will run for President from whatever prison he's in at the time?

Lyndon has run as both a Democrat and an Independent, and wants to build a city on Mars. Then there's perennial George Washington America (original name, Assan Romieh) of New York City, who will run on any ticket, and who wants to devise a "human face system" for America (whatever that may be). Mr. America proclaims himself "America's greatest thinker," and in fact has sued George Bush for $6 billion on slightly less-than-substantial grounds. And there's Billy Joe Clegg, who ran on the Republican ticket in New Hampshire this year, where he listed Jesus Christ as his official spokesman. And then, of course, there's William Knaus.

Remember William Knaus from the 1992 election? He ran as the Archonist Party candidate. Knaus, a transvestite (aka Cheryl Andrea Bruhn), ran what he called a "McKinley-style campaign" from his front porch in Mendota Heights, Minnesota (in other words, he didn't feel like leaving his house). Knaus defines himself as a "lesbian oriented transsexual without romantic interest in men," which, best I can figure it, makes him among the world's few male lesbians. He is also an anti-Semite and is intensely opposed to conscription: "In the event of conscription for a pro-Zionist purpose, we shall institute the 'Klinger Plan,' where our advisees will assume the guise of lesbian-oriented transsexuals, in lesbian hang-outs, in the company of pro-Archonist, anti-Zionist lesbians."

I mean, this guy actually *ran*. Is this a great country or what?

33

DISSENSION AT GROUND ZERO

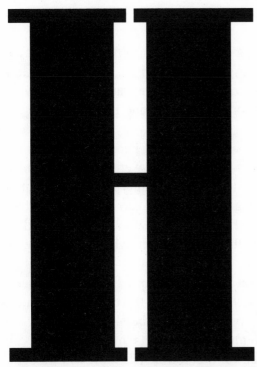

aving immersed myself in national politics for the sake of this book, I realized that I should probably take a trip down to Washington, D.C., to see the city where all this fun originates. I hadn't been to our nation's political ground zero since the seventh grade, when my teacher took us there on a class trip. Mrs. Gardino took us to the Smithsonian, the White House, the Supreme Court, and to Congress, where we watched Howard Metzenbaum decay for a few hours. It was fun, but in truth I didn't really appreciate it.

This summer, I drove down to D.C. with my wife and kids for a couple of days. It's only about a five-hour ride from New York City, and I bet most New Yorkers don't realize what a nice place it is to visit. I took my kids to the Smithsonian, the White House, the Supreme Court, and yes, to Congress, where we were disappointed to discover Howard Metzenbaum gone (I guess he's finally entered his half-life phase).

As we were getting ready for the trip home on Sunday, I noticed a protest taking place in front of the Capitol. Ah, I thought — *book material*. I parked the car, conned my wife into taking the kids for hot pretzels, and headed over to the crowd.

The assembly was a protest by the People for the Ethical Treatment of Animals (PETA), who were agitating against medical testing on animals. It was your typical assortment of Sixties hippies, young radicals with earrings through their eyeballs, and the "cat lady" from every neighborhood in America (you know, those old women who live alone with 15 cats in the house).

The thing that set this apart from the typical liberal demonstration, however, was that there was a counter-demonstration going on by another liberal group: gays. See, the homosexual community supports medical testing on animals in the search for a cure for AIDS. Wow, I thought, the bitchy infighting here is gonna make protest history. The carob cakes and designer knapsacks are really going to fly. I actually considered getting a cooler of beers and my lawn chair from the trunk and tailgating awhile — you know, make a day of it. Instead I just hovered around the fringes a bit, then left.

Driving home, I had to control my glee at the prospect of two radical-left groups at each other's throats. I couldn't wait to get to my laptop. Dissension among the liberal ranks. Good stuff! This had to get its own chapter.

But by the time I hit the New York border, I had come to another realization. The homosexuals that were out there protesting were not lobbying to march in someone else's parade, or for full partner-benefits, or for the right to marry a dromedary or something. No, this gay rights protest was different. These homosexuals were simply protesting for their right to be considered more important than your average lab rat. In this instance, their position was so sensible, it was positively conservative.

Now I should point out that this is not merely a gay issue — not by any means. These PETA people are not opposed to just AIDS testing on animals. They're opposed to *all* medical testing on animals: cancer, diabetes, heart disease, you name it. Homosexuals just happen to be the group most directly impacted these days.

Look, there are all sorts of fringe groups out there that push all sorts of wacky agendas — that's a given. But this one is truly unique. There's different ways to look at any political issue; but at least politics generally deals with the welfare of our fellow citizens. These PETA people, however, don't care about *anything* with less than four legs.

Is the situation really that bad? Am I overstating this? Are there really that many lunatics out there who prefer the welfare of animals to the well-being of the human race?

The answer, of course, is — of course.

34

PETAPHILIA

'm sure like me, most of you have seen clips of PETA protests on the evening news, and have thought to yourselves, "Well, good for them. Cruelty to animals is completely out of line."

But while these PETA protestors were holding up posters of tortured or abused animals, and chanting slogans decrying the "animal holocaust" which is currently supposed to be occurring, did anyone ever tell you what PETA's full agenda consists of? My guess would be: probably not. Because if more people were aware of how PETA actually spends the donation money they get by waving those posters, the whole PETA bunch would have been plucked and roasted years ago.

A quick refresher on some of PETA's activities: this is the gang that throws red paint on people wearing fur coats, that breaks into medical labs to free lab mice, that frees lobsters from fishermen's traps, and so on. Their biggest media moment may have been when talk show host/weight loss experiment Ricki Lake joined them in protesting at a Manhattan office building in 1994. Lake was arrested, and the incident received widespread coverage, launching PETA into the national consciousness.

The whole thing, naturally, was about as spontaneous as a shuttle launch. Lake and her fellow protesters barged into the office of fashion designer Karl Lagerfeld and plastered his walls with anti-fur decals and posters (Lagerfeld's fashion line includes furs). Now don't get me wrong — my level of concern for the fashion world matches my interest in Scandinavian tidal charts. But whether you're for fur or against it, when you consider that Ricki made sure the protest occurred during sweeps week, I think you'll agree that ol' Karl here, got screwed.

Now what first came to mind upon hearing of Ricki's new found "animal passion" was a little film called *Pink Flamingos*, directed by cult fave John Waters. Ever heard of him? For those of you who are not fans of high culture, let me fill you in.

From as early as 1988, Ricki Lake has been among the tight-knit group of off-beat actors and filmmakers involved with director Waters. Lake has starred in a bunch of Waters's movies, including the recent hit *Serial Mom* in 1994. Waters tends to use the same group of actors and actresses for most of his movies; Ricki is solidly placed on the director's A-list.

One of Waters's most notorious films is a bit of Oscar-bait titled *Pink Flamingos* (1972). Made for what looks to be about forty dollars, and shot in grainy black and white, *Flamingos* includes some of the most disturbing and tasteless scenes ever filmed (a 300-pound transvestite eating dog excrement, homosexual incest, cannibalism, etc.).

Probably the most jarring, however, is a scene where a man violently rapes a woman with a live chicken. The chicken is kicking, screeching, and bleeding. The woman ain't too happy either. Needless to say, the authorities freaked over the incident, but Waters jokingly dismisses the controversy, explaining that the cast later ate the chicken (the chicken clearly dies during the scene). *

So how is it that Ricki Lake, a woman who felt free to trash Karl Lagerfeld's office, can work so closely with a director who shot a "love" scene featuring a man, a woman, and a *very* agitated chicken? Obviously, for the same reason she could appear on David Letterman following the Lagerfeld episode wearing leather gloves. Let's face it, Ricki would dress up like a chicken and flap around Times Square if it would guarantee her a 12 share (which it probably would, actually).

---

* Not that eating the chicken would make PETA any happier; the group is firmly against the consumption of any animal by humans (it's okay for an *animal* to eat an animal, however). Incidentally, PETA is also totally opposed to human consumption of any dairy products, including milk, cheese, eggs, and butter. (I bet you didn't realize that your last slice of pizza made you guilty of "species-ism," and a co-conspirator in the worldwide animal holocaust.)

But this sort of thing is typical of PETA. For instance, in 1994 the group recruited six supermodels to appear on billboard ads that stated, "We'd rather go naked than wear fur." I have to wonder whether the models (including Cindy Crawford, Naomi Campbell, and Tyra Banks) realized that along with *fur*, PETA calls for a ban on clothes made of *silk* (because of "cruelty" to silkworms). So guess what girls? It looks like you *are* going to have to go naked after all (Stop! That doesn't apply to you, Ricki). And besides: Is there anyone out there who would actually change their opinion based on what a *supermodel* thinks?

PETA is just full of hidden or under-publicized agendas, but for some reason the group still attracts bird-brained celebrities like a Mike Ovitz beach party. Other big names on the PETA celebrity list: Woody Harrelson, Jason Priestly, Bea Arthur, Liza Minnelli, Todd Oldham, Paul McCartney, k.d. Lang, Tippi Hedren, Rue McLanahan, Kim Bassinger, Alec Baldwin, and the husband and wife team of Kirstie Alley and Parker Stevenson, who also wanted to appear in the "We'd rather go naked ..." ads. Apparently, PETA had to draw the line somewhere.

PETAPHILES AMOK

After my encounter with PETA in D.C., I decided to do some research to see if their stance on animal testing was really as extreme as those protesters were saying. And you know what? It's *worse*. You wouldn't believe some of the things that PETA wants. For instance, they could only be against *cruel or unnecessary* medical testing, right? Wrong. These people really do want to ban *all* testing on animals.

Now, allow me to add a qualifier here. I don't believe we should use animals to test non-essential items, like cosmetics and such. I don't think animals should suffer and die just so we can have a better breed of glitter eye-shadow. And I should also point out that I *like* animals. Realistically, who doesn't? As I've already said, I have a dog (or he has me — I'm not sure how it's worked out). And let's face it, with animal-testing not nearly regulated enough, all types of repetitive and unnecessary medical tests must occur. These are legitimate concerns, and I agree that they should be addressed.

But even solving these problems isn't enough to appease PETA. These characters want to ban *all* testing on animals, regardless of its benefits or the conditions that it's conducted under. And that's not humane or even inhumane; it's inhuman.

See, PETA's position, which ignores medical history (and basic logic), is that medical testing just does not work. Dismissing the opinions of such right-wing fringe groups as the American Cancer Society and the American Heart Association (as well as 50 other medical groups), PETA claims that animal testing has *never* helped advance medicine.

Newly-emerging medical genius and B-movie tart Linda Blair sums up PETA's position on this issue brilliantly: "We have been doing research on animals, which do get cancer, for 30 years with no cure in sight. Why would anyone think that a cure for AIDS can be found in testing on animals when they do not get HIV?" Um, Linda? Maybe because evidence indicates AIDS may have *come* from monkeys? (And even more obvious, why would anyone take the opinion of a child actor turned soft-core extra on matters of medical import?).

After taking into account the diagnosis of the celebrated Dr. Blair, I was prepared to list a number of medical advances made through animal research to refute her ingenious hypothesis (*including* advances in cancer and AIDS treatment). But it turns out that I don't have to bother, because it really doesn't matter. See, PETA doesn't care if animal testing *does* work. They *still* think it should be illegal. PETA manager Linda Lange: "Animal research is not going to find a cure for AIDS. And we'd be opposed to it anyway because we always take the animal's side of the case."

Now, I have to just say: Of all the freakazoid looney-tunes I've paid tribute to in this humble little tome, this woman is queen of the funhouse follies. She is actually saying that if it's necessary to kill an animal in order to save a person, it's not worth it — the animal is more important. This goes beyond extremism; this is actually *frightening*. I mean, was this woman raised by wolves or something? These activists have essentially become the ultimate race traitors, willing to sell out the *human* race for the sake of a few stupid rodents.

But are they sincere? Let me pose a hypothetical. If I held a .44 magnum to this very strange woman's head, and another gun to the head of a lab rat, and told her to pick my victim — what do you think she'd do? (Remember to bet with your head, not your heart). I mean, she *did* say she always sides with the animals ...

Now I don't know that scientists are going to cure AIDS through testing on animals, but I do know one thing. If I had AIDS, I sure as hell would want them trying. And if Ricki Lake, Woody Harrelson, or any giggly supermodel interfered, I would threaten to start medical testing on *them*.

WHEN DOES PETA SEASON OPEN?

I think it's important to remember that there are many legitimate groups out there who are helpful to animals — you just have to be sure who you're giving money to. And with PETA, you can never really be sure just what they're doing. Did I tell you their agenda was a bit on the psychotic side? Well, it just keeps on coming. Because the wonderful world of PETA also includes a total ban on hunting and fishing. A *total* ban.

Now, I know as much about hunting and fishing as I do about quantum mechanics. But somehow, this particular proposal doesn't exactly strike me as feasible. Let's forget the 81,000 Americans who would immediately lose their jobs if PETA had their way. And let's forget the billions of people worldwide who would starve to death if they couldn't eat animals or fish.

What makes this one so contradictory is: What about the animals themselves? It's a pretty basic concept that animal populations are regulated by hunting; otherwise, many animal species would overpopulate and a large percentage would starve to death. Let's face it, if all hunting immediately stopped, there would be caribou in my living room by next month (which is something you generally don't see outside of Bombay). Does PETA have some magic answer for this? Is Ricki ready to put a 1500-pound kudu up in her Malibu guest house?

But you know what? I shouldn't have to justify our consumption of meat by saying that it's all for the good of animals. Let's face it, that's not really the reason people enjoy a good barbecue. And after all, animals themselves certainly don't seem very conscience-stricken when they're chomping on each other. Why is it that because we're the creatures at the top of the food chain, we're the ones not invited to dinner? Do these PETA people think that if a bunch of lions figured out a way to domesticate and raise human beings, they wouldn't immediately institute The Wilt Chamberlain stud farm?

For their own purposes, PETA is essentially asking us to refute our natural place in the world (for better or worse, we have the superior intelligence — if Ricki Lake got left out, that's too bad). And as the Earth's primary intellects, we *should* take responsibility towards animals — it's only right. I just think we're also entitled to use that intelligence to invent new and exciting shishkabob marinades.

THROW ANOTHER SUPERMODEL ON THE BARBIE

You know, I could never understand why animal rights groups in the past were opposed to hunting but not to fishing. What makes your average bush pig more valuable than a Pacific blue marlin? Well apparently someone over in the PETA camp finally noticed. Because in late 1995, PETA decided it was time to put a stop to the "aquatic agony" caused by the world's $39 billion fishing industry (my previous idea of "aquatic agony" had been *Blue Lagoon II*, but whatever).

Calling it the "final frontier for the animal rights movement," PETA's first act in the fish campaign was to try to install a "Fish Amnesty Day" on the fourth Saturday in September. "We want

> Hoo, hoo, hoo, hoo ... **hoo, hoo, hoo, hoo** ... wah, wah wah — **WWWAAAAAUUUGGGHHHH!!!**
> — Chimp specialist Jane Goodall, opening her speech at the 3rd Annual March for the Animals with a chimpanzee greeting that "began softly and built to a near scream."

there to be one day when fish are able to swim freely and without fear," explained PETA's Tracy Reiman (gee, Tracy, I have noticed my goldfish developing a bit of a nervous tic). And in their attempt to create a fearless world for fish everywhere, PETA members have taken to disrupting fishing tournaments by throwing rocks at the water to scare fish away. Is it me, or is *scaring* fish away in order to let them "swim without *fear*" just a trifle inconsistent?

Lobsters are fascinating beings with complex social interactions, long childhoods and awkward adolescences. Like humans, they flirt with one another and have even been seen walking "claw-in-claw"! — Mary Tyler Moore

Now as I've already said, I don't support unnecessary cruelty to animals, that's wrong. For instance, I read that the orangutan used in Clint Eastwood's film *Every Which Way But Loose* was beaten to death on the set. Obviously, that's just terrible. Besides, if they're going to start killing bad actors, PETA will lose half its membership. But that aside, I think someone has to tell these PETA characters that on a planet where millions starve, the chances of the human race suddenly deciding to ignore one of its primary food sources is about equal to the chance Madonna's kid has of growing up normal.

SORRY MISTER CHEETAH, BUT YOU'RE UNDER ARREST: PETA AND NON-HUMAN RIGHTS

Okay. Up until now these PETA characters have been displaying what I'll generously call, "stupidity beyond all redemption." But we are now about to enter the realm of the surreal. Ready?

Have you heard about "non-human rights"? This theory is the basic foundation of PETA's ideology, and let me tell you, it's really *out there.*

Basically, it boils down to this. According to the current legal set-up, animals have no real "rights" of their own. Now, that doesn't mean you can use your neighbor's dog to hone your dart game; there are laws set up against such cruelty. But in the eyes of American law, animals are only considered *property.* Animals can't sue, they don't vote, and last I saw, they can't drink in bars (although you'd never know that from a few of the items I brought home in college).

PETA, on the other hand, has a different idea about all this. It is the basic philosophy of this group that animals should receive rights that are *commensurate with those humans enjoy.* In other words, you would have to treat any animal you see with the same deference that you apply

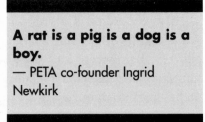

A rat is a pig is a dog is a boy.
— PETA co-founder Ingrid Newkirk

to people. You wouldn't be able to cage one, you wouldn't be able to own one, and you certainly wouldn't be able to eat one. Animals would have every bit the same amount of self-determination as humans. Have you stopped laughing yet?

You know who this is most cruel to? Animals. That's right. If suddenly humans were not allowed to determine the course of any animal's life, do you realize what absolute anarchy would ensue? The road pizza would be an inch thick on every street in America. Dogs and cats would be wandering around confused as hell, domesticated species like pigs and horses would starve or turn on each other, and as for the human animal, well, we'd be up to our asses in horseshit. As we are right now, with this theory of non-human rights.

Now obviously this is just plain stupid, and I apologize for wasting your time explicating this concept (but hey, that's the fun of this book). The problem here is that the PETA people don't really understand "rights," or if they do, they're choosing ignorance. See, humans receive rights because we are part of a basic social contract that also saddles us with responsibilities. If we break the contract, our rights are taken away: it's called law. How the hell are animals going to be part of a social contract? They're not even part of society. They're *animals* for God's sake! They can't be part of *any* agreement! Most dogs I've known would *eat* the contract before even *considering* having their lawyer review it for loopholes.

Now I'll admit I'm no anthropologist, so maybe I'm wrong. And while *I* certainly can't handle it, maybe we can get Alec Baldwin or k.d. Lang to negotiate with the animal kingdom for us; maybe they can get the animals to understand this concept of rights and responsibilities, and cut us a deal. I want to do my part, so I've compiled a few ideas for our animal mediation team to bring to the table. Alec, you can tell the animals that this is our offer:

— We humans will stop trying to make dogs look at themselves in the mirror if they will stop licking their testicles in front of our in-laws;

— We will stop putting cats out of the house at night if they agree to tone down their 4:00 am concertos;

— We will stop eating Mako sharks if they will stop trying to eat us;

— We will stop testing medicine on rats if they will relinquish control of the New York City subway system;

— We will stop eating cows if they will stop screwing up the ozone with their nuclear flatulence;

— We will stop eating bacon if pigs will stop seeing their own crap as a fashion accessory.

We will also have to let lions and cheetahs know that they can no longer treat wildebeests like the fast food of the Serengeti, and that Indiana tourists should not be considered holiday delicacies.

THEY FEEL YOUR DISHWASHER'S PAIN:
NON-HUMAN RIGHTS AROUND THE HOUSE

The funniest part of this non-human rights theory is that it does not require rights-recipients to meet any human criteria whatsoever. For instance, the animals are not required to have rational thought or to know how to polka or to find Richard Simmons ridiculous. No, the animals would be granted these rights essentially because PETA finds animals cute. This rather expansive theory begs the question: Why just animals? Why not rocks? Rivers? Trees?... Trees, you say?

In 1993 the New York zoological Society decided that the word "zoo" had become derogatory, and so replaced the word "zoo" with "Conservation Center." The Society feared that in modern usage, "zoo" had taken on a secondary meaning connoting a place where chaos reigns. Apparently the New York Zoological Society changed the word because they were concerned about their reputation; they didn't want the public to think that the New York Conservation Centers had turned into ... well, zoos.

In his book *Should Trees Have Standing* (considered a classic in the environmental world), respected UCLA law professor Christopher Stone argues that natural objects should have rights of their own. Stone contends that our world would be better off if we granted trees, rivers, and rocks these same non-human rights. Rocks? Hey sure, why not? I like rocks. Rocks, trees, dogs, yaks. Hell, why not my dishwasher? Dishwashers, you say?

In 1988 two "Strategic Planners/Futurists" employed by the Hawaii Judiciary presented a report to the Hawaii Supreme Court that argued for *robot rights*:

As we enter a post-industrial, technology-driven society, we need to reassess our interconnected relationship with nature and machines as well as the notion of rights associated with this new relationship ... Perhaps what we really need to do is to rewrite the Constitution in the light of future trends and issues ... The Constitution could be rewritten to include the rights of trees and streams, robots and humans.

Robots? Machines? They want to give my laser printer rights? I haven't even figured out how to work the thing yet! You give it rights and it'll probably run away with my microwave.

So now you see where the PETA gang is leading us. I'm sure Ricki Lake never bothered to think through the fact that her little ratings stunt might eventually lead to a dishwasher or VCR petitioning for the vote or for affirmative action benefits.

Well I'll tell you one thing. If robots ever do get the vote, we all know what party they're likely to join. How long until a clever little Macintosh PowerBook is the "guest of honor" at Renaissance Weekend?

CONSERVATISM IN ACTION — 25 REASONS I'M A REPUBLICAN

t doesn't feel like it's moving — why isn't it moving?... No, I don't know why the elevator's stopped, Miss Streisand. I guess we're stuck ... I really don't know how to fix it, Miss Streisand, looks like we're trapped here ... What are you doing? No, Miss Streisand, please, no ... I'm a married man, Miss Streisand! Please, no ... Oh lord, someone help me! Please, nooooooooooo ...

Huh? Oh thank God! It was only a nightmare, and I lay staring at the ceiling a moment, relieved beyond words (1). But then I remember it's Monday morning, and I'm up and out of bed and into the shower. I brush my teeth with regular toothpaste; I don't like the taste or feel of baking soda in my mouth, and I couldn't care less if this is the latest "natural" way to clean teeth (2). Besides, I haven't had a cavity in years.

Breakfast — ahh, a special time for any conservative. I haven't had to head out into the jungle yet, I'm still at home, in the bosom of family and domicile. My wife cooks breakfast for all of us, and not because I *make* her, but because she *chooses* to; luckily, we can live on my salary, and neither of us wastes any time in thinking she's "oppressed" because she's decided not to work while the kids are young (3). Breakfast is a right-wing tour-de-force; scrambled eggs, buttered toast, and even some bacon, and if possible, I'd tell my wife that I'd like extra cholesterol with that, thank you (4).

The Sunday *New York Times* still lies scattered around the kitchen, but I feel no compunction about ignoring it or today's edition of the "paper of record" (5); which is convenient, as conservative or liberal, is there anything more cumbersome than trying to read the *Times* while doing anything? It only seems possible to read those big spreadsheets if you're seated alone at a draftsman's table.

Instead, I watch television. In our kitchen a little TV is perched on the counter, and I'm in my glory as I sit talking back at the screen, making fun of Bryant Gumbel's tie and his paralyzed attempts at wit (6), all the while pounding down at least two big mugs of extra dense coffee, injecting enough caffeine into my system to jump start a bullet train (7).

My body primed, I slip into a suit that may or may not have been made in a sweatshop; I don't agonize over it. Not that I *support* sweatshops, I just don't lose any time out of my day on guilt trips over a situation that, realistically, I am in no way responsible for (8). You think I have time to investigate my underwear? I have to wear clothes, don't I? This isn't Venice Beach.

The kids already out to school, I kiss the wife goodbye and head to my car, a big, safe, American battleship of a vehicle that should have its own zip code (9). Starting this behemoth up, I switch on the radio, and am immediately soothed by the dulcet strains of my local AM radio talk-personality (10), who if possible has even less tolerance than I do for designer-liberalism and its media propagandists. I've been told this sort of thing is rabble-rousing; but who you calling rabble, pal? I can almost hear the veins popping in this announcer's neck as he blares away, and I break into unreserved howls at nearly every observation he makes. Life is good.

Believe it or not, I'm one of those characters who actually enjoys what he does for a living, and arriving at work, I feel like I'm settling in with an old friend. I work at, for want of a better term, a "financial institution," and arriving at a company founded on and committed to the profit motive feels to me like a regular homecoming (11). Nobody here worries if the complex transactions of the day may be insulting to the Inuit or damaging to the habitat of the North American coatimundi — at work, with money and self-interest at stake, liberalism lifts like a vapor, and people are finally themselves, greedy sons-a-bitches all. Thank God.

I spend the day at my desk or at various activities, including a lot of time on the phone. I take notes on thick sheets of crisp, white, non-recycled paper, instead of that crappy gray stuff Al Gore wants us to use (12). That way every jotting of mine leaves me with the warm glow that I'm contributing to the health of America's timber industry. While I do all this, I occasionally note office temps and messengers arriving with documents and such — and I happily steal appraising glances at the women among them, dressed as they are in prim office finery and looking elegant and seductive at the same time. Sexual harassment? I don't think so (13) (sure I'm married, but I can *look* sometimes, can't I? I mean, I've got a few functioning hormones left). Meanwhile, I write a report at my desk, using the general pronoun "he," and not wasting a lick of thought over my role in furthering the gender-bias of the English language (14). When women write, *they* can use the "she" — that seems fair, doesn't it?

Lunch time! I head out into the teeming city streets, passing "bistros" and "grilleries" of all sorts, and head for a local greasy spoon, an alleyway establishment owned by an old army cook and featuring a cast of characters out of a Scorsese movie. I order a cheeseburger, extra cheese, and I can feel freedom singing in my veins as I tell the waitress I'll have a chocolate shake with that (15). I don't have a weight problem — why should I worry about other people's chin count?

One thing I like about that little burger joint — it's quick. It's barely twenty minutes later that I'm back on the street, looking to kill a half-hour or so. What better time for a quick trim? I head to the barber (not a *hairstylist*) (16), and a guy who looks like an extra from *On The Waterfront* dispassionately snips at my unruly locks, all the while sucking an unfiltered cigarette that must have his lungs looking like the interior of a locomotive. Hey, that's *his* business.

The rest of my workday goes much the same, and it seems I'm barely back from lunch when it's time to head home. Then, sitting on the crowded subway, I do the unthinkable — I get out of my seat and offer it to a woman holding a couple of shopping bags (17). It's a risky move; I once had a woman berate me so forcefully for this, I got off at the next stop and ended up the sole English-speaker in a neighborhood I'd never seen before. I can feel all eyes in the car on us now as she nods a thanks and sits down. I have once again contributed to society's perceptions of gender-bias — how un-P.C. can you get?

Standing now, I kill some time reading as the train blasts me out of Manhattan towards home. My literature of choice? A little masterpiece called *The Killer Inside Me*, by a no-nonsense guy named Jim Thompson, who may not be righting the wrongs of the world but who knows how to move a plot forward better than half these characters with Pulitzer prizes (18). Besides, Thompson always includes a few guns, a femme fatale or two, and a plot-twist that leaves you with a wrenched neck. Too bad Margaret Atwood can't say the same.

I arrive home in my steamship of a car after the second leg of my commute, feeling like a conquering Viking returning from a raid. At the door I'm greeted by my dog, who is never less than ecstatic to see me. He's a mutt, and looks it, with shaggy hair and a big, bushy tail — and who I wouldn't have "groomed" or "sculpted" at gunpoint (19).

I can already smell dinner cooking, as inviting an aroma as there is for anyone returning from a day's work, and I'm pleased to be told by my wife that tonight it's pork chops, another in a long history of non-P.C. meals devoid of sprouts or anything labeled "organic" (20). We spend a satisfying dinner talking about my kids' day at school, and as usual I wonder why they don't have more homework.

I have a little time to myself afterwards, so I plop down contentedly in front of the television. While I'm not a huge television fan, I do enjoy "channel-surfing", and I get particular kicks clicking by such liberal soapboxes as PBS and CNN. What could be more fun than waiting until Cornell West is going to self-importantly respond to Charlie Rose's question, and then clicking over to the Discovery Channel at that precise moment (21)? *I'll* tell you what — watching the Discovery Channel for only those few seconds when the lion is bringing down that big gazelle (22). As soon as that's done, and we get into the sleeping habits of the great wild mongoose, it's time to head over to ESPN.

There's still a bit of daylight left, and I feel like getting some air, so I spend an hour or so on our driveway firing street-hockey pucks at my oldest, who for reasons known only to himself harbors dreams of being a goalie. I wouldn't even attempt to rollerblade, but I love hockey, and so do my kids, the violence be damned (23), and my kids fly around on in-line skates like they were born on wheels. I only wish they had them when I was a kid.

Later, after working at my computer awhile, I spend late night in front of the TV again, this time with the wife, just the two of us. Generally we look for a movie or something, or even rent one from the video store; but who can be bothered on a Monday night? And as there's no good movies on anywhere, we end up watching the late-night talk shows, where a parade of stand-up comics engage in a liberal pander-fest worthy of an Academy Awards acceptance speech. I get a vicarious thrill out of feeling like the only person alive who sees these smirking oafs for what they are (24). Rather than attempts at cleverness, they generally go for the typical stand-up comic's routine: denounce a well-known conservative as unhip or corrupt, then wait as the be-guilted audience bursts into less-than-spontaneous applause. Is this lame tactic part of the stand-up comic's handbook or something?

And then, the kids asleep and the dog walked, I lie in bed and experience one of those moments when one feels as if the world is spinning in its proper orbit. My wife and kids are healthy, my job seems secure, and I even have a few bucks left over for a vacation this year. So as another day ends uneventfully, I again do the unthinkable, and say a little prayer that it all stays that way (25). So far, it has; I must be doing something right.

POP QUIZ: ARE YOU A CLOSET LIBERAL?

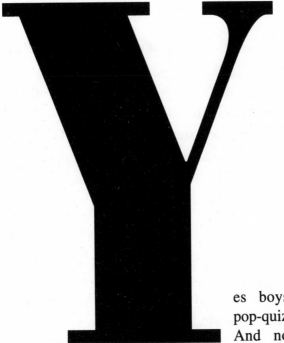

es boys and girls, pop-quiz time again! And now that the book is almost over, time to discover a little something about yourself. Today's topic: Are you a closet liberal?

Now just because you find this Franken guy ridiculous doesn't mean you're on the "right" side of the fence — *if* you know what I mean! So just respond to these questions with brutal honesty — then check the answers to see if you've been watching too much *60 Minutes*!

1. When I go to the movies, I generally like to see films directed by

   a. Spike Lee,
   b. Rob Reiner,
   c. Oliver Stone,
   d. Russ Meyer.

2. When I go to a restaurant, one of the things I generally do is

   a. ask if the "oven-braised asparagus" is "organically grown and pesticide-free,"
   b. ask if the "seared tuna steak" is "dolphin-safe,"
   c. send back the "broasted chicken breast" because it doesn't taste "free-range" enough,
   d. eat.

3. My idea of an enjoyable weekend activity is

   a. sitting in front of the television with the VCR remote, ready to tape any and all appearances by/mentions of an American hero — Mr. Ed Asner,
   b. raiding the video store and having my own little Merchant-Ivory film festival,
   c. working on my oil painting masterpiece, *Still Life With Tipper,*
   d. handicapping midget wrestling.

4. I believe the new one hundred dollar bills should have pictured

   a. William Kunstler,

   b. Karl Marx,

   c. Mary Steenburgen,

   d. Elvis.

Correct
Answers: d   Now grade yourself:

4 out of 4 right: True-blue member of the silent majority;

3 out of 4 right: Well-intentioned, but can be guilted into tai-chi lessons with the spouse;

2 out of 4 right: Clintonista — liberal at movie openings, conservative during election years;

1 out of 4 right: Approaching the fringe — a beret short of an *apparatchik;*

0 out of 4 right: Alan Alda.

37

IN DEFENSE OF GOD, COUNTRY, AND IMUS

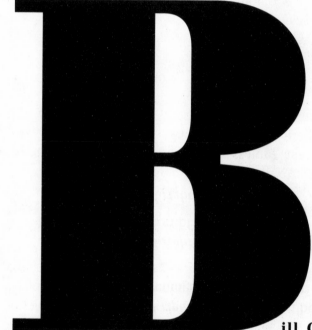

" **B** ill Clinton:

Greatest President of the Twentieth Century."

Unless you count the first 92 years.

In a mental spasm of John DuPont proportions, Al Franken actually penned that first line in his book. Al, this is 1996 — isn't it time you stopped drinking the bong water?

This is not to say that Bill Clinton hasn't achieved several important milestones. For instance, who could forget his being the only President to throw out the first pitch of baseball season and actually reach home plate? I swear, I got *chills*.

Alright, Clinton has done one or two decent things, I'll give him that. Let's not be stingy. But realistically, what President hasn't? A certain number of decent things are bound to happen to *any* politician. Even Jerry Brown managed to get a bill through once (I think). But in the final analysis, Bill Clinton will never be considered a "great" President because he took office at a time when the U.S. was unquestionably the biggest kid on the block. And since 1992 we've had no *real* pressing concerns (remember I'm speaking relative to other Presidents here).

Forget bi-partisan loyalties for a moment — just think about it. Largely due to the Reagan years (see Chapter 15), Clinton inherited a country that was devoid of any real outside threat (unless of course you consider the re-emergence of Yakoff Smirnoff a renewed Russian threat). Let's consider it comparatively. For the first forty-five years or so, U.S. Presidents in the twentieth century had to deal with a highly-militarized, insanely-belligerent Germany set on exterminating the "inferior races," expanding its territories, and eventually ruling the world; for the second forty-five years or so, they had to deal with a dangerously nuclear and devotedly expansionist U.S.S.R. capable of obliterating the entire planet at the behest of one vodka-soaked cossack. During the Clinton years, the most significant threat to U.S. security has been a highly militarized, dangerously expansionist Montana Militia determined to avoid taxes and marry their sisters. I'm sorry, but until the North Koreans come screaming over the DMZ en masse, I'm just not impressed.

Now I'll admit that the job of President is never easy. But

I don't care what side of the aisle your view is from, this is just stupid. I mean, what the hell is Franken so impressed by? Al has either lost his mind or he's on the White House payroll, because this isn't political humor he's pitching any more, this is *propaganda*. Hey Al, was your comedy career going that badly?

But by becoming the Democrat's version of a Moonie, Al has actually performed a service for us; he's set himself up as the perfect metaphor for all the typical phoniness that goes with designer liberalism. I'll show you what I mean.

In his book, Franken writes about the 1976 appearance of Gerald Ford's Press Secretary Ron Nessen on *Saturday Night Live*. As an SNL writer, Franken and the cast of the show had been tweaking Ford for weeks about his "stumblebum" reputation. Nessen hosted the show, hoping to take the wind out of those sails. It didn't work. On that show not only did the cast parody Ford as a bumbling oaf, but they presented some of the most daring and cutting material they ever aired. They embarrassed Nessen, Ford, and the whole administration. Franken was in on some of the writing, and it was one hilarious show.

But these days Franken has a new schtick. At the White House Correspondents Dinner in May of this year, Franken harangued radio talk-show host Don Imus relentlessly because Imus had *dared* to satirize Bill Clinton at a similar event back in March. The photo that ran in the papers the next day showed a beaming Al Franken getting a handshake from the President, looking for all the world like a seal getting a herring from its trainer.

Al, you hypocritical little dick! Don't you remember what this comedy thing is all about? Don't you remember what you did to the Ford administration in '76? And to the Carter administration after that?

It seems Franken's memory is getting as selective as his targets. At least when Don's turn came he was a bi-partisan offender, roundly digging into everyone in the room for laughs, regardless of party. And then two months later, Franken spends his act attacking Imus for doing what Al himself has made an entire *career* of doing?

I mean, how liberal can you get?

38
EPILOGUE

o this bizarre emergence of Al Franken as the left's new scourge on conservatism is what prompted me to write this book. Frankly, the concept of a guy who used to answer to Chevy Chase now collecting on a bestseller was enough to make me consider cryogenically freezing myself for a few decades.

But as I sat there on the E-train, heading home from my regular job the day before my final manuscript was due, I began to ponder on all the things I wrote about Franken and the Democrats. All the teeth and Ted Kennedy jokes, all the Al Gore-is-a-stiff and Hillary jabs, all the Carville and Stephanopoulos shots.

And you know what? I began to feel twinges of remorse. I began to think maybe the Democrats and liberals *are* right about some things. Maybe even a lot of them. I mean, what do I really know? Maybe affirmative action *isn't* dehumanizing. Maybe we *should* revise the history curriculum. Maybe there *is* nothing wrong with big government. And maybe they're not all as pompous and hypocritical as they appear. Could it be that I just don't trust anyone since Miss Thibadeau, hippy educator and breaker of fourth-graders' hearts?

I sat contemplating this, with a rising feeling somewhat like motion sickness, until I realized my eyes were resting on the back of a *New York Times* the woman across from me was reading. And suddenly, there was the truth, all laid out for me.

All I had to do was scan the headlines as she turned the pages. There was Bill Clinton back-pedaling on trade negotiations with China just to avoid making waves in an election year. There was another liberal judge turning a killer loose up in the Bronx. There was another editorial portraying prominent Republicans as dupes and racists because they actually support police. And of course, there was the inevitable *Times* story proclaiming how four more years of Bill Clinton is already a foregone conclusion.

But that wasn't the worst. Because as my train pulled in at my stop, in a city I love but have diminishing hopes for, and I got up to leave the sooty confines of the New York

City subway system, I saw that Franken's book was still resting comfortably on the *Times* bestseller list.

The horror ...

After that, there could be no doubt. I realized yet again, with the consummate solace of embracing Truth,

"You know, Al Franken *is* a bucktoothed moron."

INDEX

ABOUT THE REAL AUTHORS

J.P. Mauro is a composite character created by brothers Joseph and Paul Mauro for the purpose of writing this book.

Joseph Mauro is a New York attorney and writer who has published articles in *The New York Law Journal*, as well as other legal journals. He is also the former humor editor for *First Amendment Publishing*.

Paul Mauro is a New York writer and ex-editor of *National Lampoon*. A former university English professor, he has published numerous articles in a variety of publications.

Editor's note: To avoid the confusion that accompanied Mr. Franken's book, allow me to clarify:

Chapter 1, "The Mauro-Franken Letters," is fake.

Chapter 11, "My Very Own Deep Throat," occurred as described.

Chapter 24, "My Search for Jesse Jackson's Job," occurred as described.

The Artists
Chapter 3, "Franken Fever — *Catch It!*", and
Chapter 21, "The Bimbo Patrol Rides Again!"
  illustrations by Jared Phillips.
All other illustrations by Frank Cummings.

The authors wish to thank the following people:
Jay and Karen Murtha, for edits, conversation, and desperately-needed foodstuffs; Cathy Hanley, for sharp suggestions and tea-on-demand; Maurice Kamhi, for sage advice and support throughout; Ron Wilcox for crispy burritos and his patented wildebeestisms; the Mighty Shaker, for taking time out from rollerblading to provide a thoughtful opposing viewpoint; Barbara Silber, the human spell-check, for eagle-eyed edits; Karen Hanley for needed support, excellent recommendations, and not a few punchlines; Gerard Hanley for catching that extra comma; Danny Muro for patience and design expertise; Jay Kamhi for faith; and of course Mom and Dad, for years of support without once suggesting the Foreign Legion.